THE COLD WAR

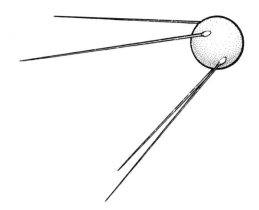

THE COLD WAR
A MILITARY HISTORY

Lawrence Freedman

General Editor: John Keegan

CASSELL&**CO**

Cassell & Co
Wellington House, 125 Strand
London WC2R 0BB

First published 2001

British Library Cataloguing-in-Publication Data
A catalogue record for this book is available from the
British Library.
ISBN 0-304-35290-X

Cartography: Arcadia Editions
Picture research: Elaine Willis
Design: Martin Hendry

Typeset in Monotype Sabon

ACKNOWLEDGEMENTS

I have been working on Cold War issues since I started postgraduate work almost three decades ago. Since 1982 I have been at the Department of War Studies at King's College, London, which has proved throughout to be a stimulating and congenial environment. I am indebted not only to my colleagues but also to my students for their searching questions and, in many cases, their own studies. This particular book has been driven forward by Penny Gardiner, who has not let me slack and with whom it has been great fun to work. I must also thank Elaine Willis, for her ability to find even the most obscure of picture requests, and Malcolm Swanston for his inventiveness and creativity in the mapmaking.

LAWRENCE FREEDMAN
London

In a favourite North Vietnamese image, a small member of the People's Militia with a large captured American airman.

CONTENTS

KEY TO MAPS

Military units

XX
armoured division

XX
motorised infantry division

Military movements

attack

retreat

air attack

clash/attack

airfield

Geographical symbols

urban area

road

railway

river

seasonal river

canal

border

bridge or pass

MAP LIST

CHRONOLOGY

1945

11 February	Churchill, Roosevelt and Stalin meet at Yalta.
13 April	Roosevelt dies and is replaced by Vice-President Truman.
9 May	Germany surrenders.
26 June	United Nations Charter signed by fifty nations in San Francisco.
16 July	First atomic bomb tested in New Mexico.
17 July	Potsdam Conference opens between Truman, Churchill and Stalin. Churchill is replaced later that month by Attlee after the British general election.
2 August	Conference concludes.
6 August	Japanese city of Hiroshima destroyed by atomic bomb.
9 August	Second atomic bomb dropped, on Nagasaki.
10 August	Emperor Hirohito decrees Japanese surrender.

1946

5 March	Churchill's 'Iron Curtain' speech at Fulton, Missouri.
June	Bernard Baruch proposes plan to give international control of atomic energy to UN Atomic Energy Commission.
30 June	USA tests atomic weapons at Bikini Atoll.

1947

February	Britain announces the return of its Palestine mandate to the UN.
12 March	Outbreak of civil war in Greece. Truman announces the containment doctrine.
5 June	Secretary of State George Marshall proposes a plan for European economic recovery.
August	Partition of India.

1948

February	Moscow condemns Tito's independent communist regime in Yugoslavia.
March	Communist regime established in Czechoslovakia.
14 May	State of Israel proclaimed. Arab armies invade.
April	Ceasefire in Indo-Pakistan War over Kashmir.
June	Stalin begins Berlin blockade.
November	Truman re-elected US president.

1949

April	Armistice between Israel and Arabs.
4 April	North Atlantic Treaty signed by twelve nations in Washington.
May	Berlin blockade ends.
August	First Soviet atomic bomb tested.
September	Federal Republic of Germany established out of American, British and French sectors; German Democratic Republic established out of Soviet sector.
October	Chinese communists gain control of the mainland; nationalists flee to Taiwan.

1950

January	USA decides to build thermonuclear (hydrogen) bomb.
25 June	North Korea invades the South.
15 September	USA lands at Inchon, cutting off North Korea's forces.
26 November	Chinese forces mount counter-offensive against UN forces in Korea.

1951

11 April	General MacArthur relieved of command in Korea.
April	European Coal and Steel Federation formed.

1952

May	Proposals to establish European Defence Community.
3 October	Britain explodes its first atomic bomb.
1 November	USA tests the first thermonuclear device at Eniwetok Atoll.
November	Dwight D. Eisenhower elected US president.

1953

5 March	Stalin dies.
27 July	Armistice signed in Korea at Panmunjon.
12 August	Soviet Union tests its first thermonuclear weapon.

1954

12 January	John Foster Dulles announces doctrine of massive retaliation.
7 May	French troops surrender to the Viet Minh at Dien Bien Phu. Geneva Conference divides Vietnam into communist North and non-communist South, and establishes Cambodia and Laos as independent states.
August	France declines to join European Defence Community.
August	USA signs defence agreement with Japan and treaty guaranteeing the security of the Republic of China (Taiwan).

September	ANZUS (Australia, New Zealand, US) Pact formed.
September	South-East Asia Treaty Organization (SEATO) established.
October	NATO agrees that West Germany can be admitted and permitted to rearm.

1955

February	Baghdad Pact signed, leading to Central Treaty Organization.
May	State treaty ends Allied occupation of Austria.
14 May	Warsaw Pact formed.

1956

February	Nikita Khrushchev makes 'secret speech' at the Twentieth Party Congress in Moscow, denouncing Stalin.
June	Polish workers' revolt suppressed.
26 July	Egyptian president Nasser nationalizes the Suez Canal.
October	Hungarians revolt against communism suppressed by Soviet troops at the start of November.
29 October	Israel invades Sinai.
5 November	British and French paratroopers land at Port Said on the Suez Canal.
November	Eisenhower re-elected president.
22 December	Britain and France withdraw from the Suez Canal and Israel from Sinai.

1957

June	Soviet Union tests the first intercontinental ballistic missile (ICBM).
4 October	Soviet Union launches the first artificial earth satellite (Sputnik 1).
8 November	Britain explodes thermonuclear weapon.

1958

June	Collapse of the Fourth Republic in France as a result of the Algerian War. Charles de Gaulle comes to power as the first president of the Fifth Republic.
August	China blockades Taiwanese islands of Quemoy and Matsu.
November	Khrushchev issues first Berlin ultimatum.

1959

1 January	Batista flees Cuba as Castro comes to power.
16 July	Moscow rescinds Sino-Soviet nuclear agreement.
September	Khrushchev visits the USA.
December	First Polaris submarine commissioned.

1960

13 February	France explodes its first atomic device.
May	U-2 spy plane shot down over the Soviet Union.
November	John Kennedy elected US president.
December	Civil war in Laos; attempted coup against Diem in South Vietnam.

1961

January	USA breaks diplomatic relations with Cuba.
12 April	Soviet cosmonaut Yuri Gagarin becomes the first man in space.
20 April	Failure of Cuban rebel invasion at the Bay of Pigs.
June	Kennedy–Khrushchev summit meeting in Vienna.
13 August	Berlin Wall constructed.
October	Soviet Union conducts the largest atmospheric nuclear test ever (56 megatons).

1962

18 March	De Gaulle announces Algerian ceasefire.
22–28 Oct.	Cuban missile crisis.
October	Sino-Indian War.
December	Nassau summit between Harold Macmillan and Kennedy agrees on the transfer of Polaris missiles to Britain.

1963

April	US–Soviet hotline established.
August	Attempt to heal rift between China and the Soviet Union fails.
5 August	Test ban treaty signed.
1 November	Diem assassinated in South Vietnamese coup.
22 November	Kennedy assassinated; Lyndon Johnson becomes president.

1964

January	US Congress passes Civil Rights Act.
2 August	Gulf of Tonkin incident.
14 October	Khrushchev removed as leader; replaced by Leonid Brezhnev and Alexei Kosygin.
16 October	First Chinese atomic test.
November	Johnson elected US president.

1965

2 March	US bombing of North Vietnam begins.
July	US combat troops into Vietnam.
August	Indo-Pakistan War over Kashmir.
30 September	Communist coup in Indonesia fails, followed by army massacres.

1966

January	Indo-Pakistan ceasefire.
January	Mao launches the Cultural Revolution.
7 March	France withdraws from NATO's Integrated Military Command.

1967

5–10 June	Six Day War between Israel and Egypt, Jordan and Syria.
17 June	China tests thermonuclear weapon.
December	NATO adopts doctrine of flexible response.

1968

31 January	Tet Offensive in Vietnam.
April	Johnson announces bombing halt in Vietnam and his withdrawal from the US presidential race.
May	Fifth Republic in France rocked by student protests.
6 June	Robert Kennedy assassinated.
1 July	Nuclear Non-Proliferation Treaty signed.
20 August	Warsaw Pact forces invade Czechoslovakia.
29 August	France tests thermonuclear weapon.
November	Richard Nixon elected US president.

1969

March	Armed clashes on Sino-Soviet border.
28 April	De Gaulle resigns as French president.
25 July	Nixon announces policy of Vietnamization at Guam.
November	Start of Strategic Arms Limitation Talks (SALT).

1970

March	Military coup in Cambodia.
May	US and South Vietnamese troops invade Cambodia.
12 August	Soviet–West German Non-Aggression Treaty.
18 November	West Germany and Poland normalize relations.

1971

May	Congress defeats the Mansfield Amendment calling for the withdrawal of US troops from Europe.
July	Nixon accepts invitation to visit China.
September	US–Soviet Nuclear Accident Agreement.
3 December	Indo-Pakistan War leads to the creation of the independent state of Bangladesh.

1972

21 February	Nixon visits China.
30 March	Start of North Vietnamese offensive in Vietnam.
10 May	Nixon orders Linebacker 1 bombing campaign.
May	Nixon visits Moscow and signs Treaty on the Limitation of Antiballistic Missiles and the Interim Agreement on the Limitation of Strategic Offensive Weapons.
8 November	Nixon re-elected US president.

December	Mutual recognition of sovereignty by East and West Germany.
18 December	Nixon orders Linebacker 2 bombing campaign in Vietnam.

1973

27 January	Vietnam ceasefire agreement.
June	Brezhnev visits the USA.
September	Conference on Security and Cooperation in Europe (CSCE) opens in Helsinki.
11 September	Marxist Chilean president Salvador Allende deposed by military coup.
October	Talks on mutual balanced force reductions open in Vienna.
6 October	Arab–Israeli (Yom Kippur) War.
7 November	War Powers Act passed in Congress.
24 December	World oil prices quadruple.

1974

April	Coup d'état in Portugal leads to independence for colonies by November.
18 May	'Peaceful' nuclear test by India.
10 August	Nixon resigns and Gerald Ford becomes US president.

1975

13 April	Civil war commences in Lebanon.
30 April	Fall of Saigon (Vietnam) and Phnom Penh (Cambodia).
1 August	Final Act of Helsinki agreements on CSCE signed.
October	40,000 Cuban troops arrive in Angola to support Marxist MPLA.

1976

April	Syrian forces intervene in Lebanon.
9 September	Death of Mao Tse-tung.
November	Jimmy Carter elected US president.

1977

6 January	Charter 77 based on CSCE accords published by dissidents in Czechoslovakia.
20 November	Anwar Sadat of Egypt flies to Israel and speaks to the Knesset.

1978

14 March	Israeli intervention in Lebanon. The Israelis leave by June.
April	Left-wing coup in Afghanistan.
17 September	'Camp David' accords between Israel and Egypt.
December	Vietnam invades Cambodia.
December	USA normalizes relations with China.

1979

15 January	The Vietnamese take Phnom Penh.
16 January	The Shah leaves Iran.
12 February	Ayatollah Khomeini takes power in Iran.
17 February	China invades Vietnam.

March	Saddam Hussein becomes president of Iraq.
4 May	Margaret Thatcher elected prime minister in Britain.
18 June	SALT II treaty signed by Carter and Brezhnev.
17 July	Somoza overthrown in Nicaragua.
26 September	CENTO dissolved.
3 November	US embassy seized in Tehran, sixty-three hostages taken.
12 December	NATO announces its decision to deploy 572 cruise and Pershing missiles in Europe.
25 December	Soviet invasion of Afghanistan.

1980

January	US Senate suspends SALT II debate.
25 April	Failure of US raid to rescue American hostages.
4 May	Tito dies in Yugoslavia.
30 August	Formation of Solidarity in Poland.
9 September	Iraq attacks Iran.
November	Ronald Reagan elected US president.

1981

20 January	Hostages released as Reagan is inaugurated.
6 October	Sadat assassinated.
November	INF (Intermediate-Range Nuclear Forces) talks open in Geneva.
13 December	Martial law declared in Poland.

1982

April	Argentine forces occupy the Falkland Islands.
6 June	Israeli troops enter Lebanon.
14 June	British forces retake the Falkland Islands.
29 June	Strategic Arms Reduction Talks (START) open in Geneva.
27 August	Withdrawal of the PLO and Syrians from Beirut.
16–19 Sept.	Christian forces massacre Palestinians in the refugee camps of Sabra and Chatilah.
10 November	Brezhnev dies and is replaced by Yuri Andropov.

1983

23 March	President Reagan announces the Strategic Defense Initiative.
September	Soviet Union shoots down a South Korean airliner over its airspace.
October	Barracks of US and French peacekeepers in Beirut destroyed by terrorists.
November	Cruise missiles arrive in Europe. Soviet negotiators leave the INF talks.
December	Negotiators leave the START talks.

1984

7 February	Multinational force leaves Beirut.
February	Andropov dies and is replaced by Konstantin Chernenko.
November	Reagan re-elected US president.

1985

10 March	Chernenko dies and is replaced by Mikhail Gorbachev.
October	Reagan and Gorbachev meet in Geneva. Arms control talks revived.

1986

25 April	Nuclear disaster at Chernobyl in the Ukraine.
11–12 Oct.	Reykjavik summit between Reagan and Gorbachev.

1987

8 December	USA and Soviet Union sign Treaty on Intermediate Nuclear Forces.

1988

20 August	Iran–Iraq ceasefire.
November	George Bush elected US president.

1989

15 February	Soviet troops complete their departure from Afghanistan.
3–4 June	Massacre of pro-democracy demonstrators in Tiananmen Square, Beijing.
14 August	Communist rule ends in Poland. Hungary opens its border with Austria.
22 December	Berlin Wall comes down and East German borders open.
December	Communist rule collapses in Czechoslovakia and Romania.
December	Bush and Gorbachev meet off Malta.

1990

11 March	Lithuania declares independence from the Soviet Union.
2 August	Iraq invades Kuwait. Sanctions imposed against Iraq. American and British forces are sent to Saudi Arabia.
3 October	Germany reunified.

1991

16 January	Gulf War opens. Completed at the end of February with the liberation of Kuwait.
1 April	Warsaw Pact annulled.
June	War begins as Slovenia and then Croatia declare independence from Yugoslavia.
21 August	Coup against Gorbachev fails.
23 October	Peace accords on Cambodia.
December	Union of Soviet Socialist Republics dissolved.

INTRODUCTION

POWER AND IDEOLOGY

EAST GERMAN AND SOVIET SOLDIERS put on protective clothing while demonstrating anti-aircraft rockets during the Warsaw Pact's Soyuz 1981 exercises in East Germany.

POWER AND IDEOLOGY

THE COLD WAR BEGAN in 1945 as the members of the coalition against Hitler's Germany started to argue about the shape of post-war Europe. It ended with the breach of the Berlin Wall in November 1989 and the collapse of European communism. Its origins can be traced back to the entry of European communism as a formidable political force with the Bolshevik Revolution of 1917. From that point on the capitalist countries of Europe all saw revolutionary Russia as a direct threat to their own internal stability. Russia assumed that they would continue to try to snuff out the revolution, as they had first sought to do by joining the side of the Whites against the Reds as the First World War ended. Even as the Nazi campaign to dominate Europe required Britain and the United States to form common cause with Russia, the surface amity always masked an unavoidable antagonism. Neither of these two incompatible social systems could prosper without undermining the other.

What turned this ideological antagonism into a cold war was the rise of Russia as not only a revolutionary state but a Great Power, with a military capacity and reach well beyond its own borders. Prior to the Second World War

As the Great Depression took hold in the capitalist world, communist predictions of a class war, even in the United States, did not seem wholly incredible. Here unemployed demonstrators run through Union Square in New York in 1930, chased by police armed with tear gas.

the country was in perpetual turmoil – with famine, forced collectivization, rapid industrialization and purges. When Hitler launched Operation Barbarossa in 1941 there was little the Russian Army could do, and if Hitler had played his cards right he might well have obtained a good proportion of the population on his side. Helped by Hitler's strategic mistakes and the fear engendered by his racial obsessions, and then taking advantage of their old dependables of a huge territory and inhospitable climate, the Russians managed first to hold the

RENDEZVOUS

German advance and then to send it into reverse. As the Red Army marched through Europe to take Berlin, it acquired a sizeable Continental empire. When the fighting stopped, and Josef Stalin began to consolidate this empire with a ruthlessness equal to that with which he had consolidated his power in Russia, his erstwhile allies felt that they had little choice but to take notice. The logic of Soviet policy seemed to be expansion, and if the Western way of life – and economic system – was to survive, then it had to be defended against a new totalitarian threat.

The Cold War soon took on the appearance of a traditional Great Power competition, with the best hope for peace lying in a balance of power rather than international law, and both sides following the familiar logic of alliance formation and arms racing. With any balance of power there is a risk that it will fail to sustain an equilibrium, that one side will find a sudden opportunity to seize the initiative. However, the risk of a hot war, at least during the late 1940s, should not be exaggerated. There was a natural reluctance on all sides to embark on yet another world war before anybody had had a chance to recover from the last. Even without nuclear weapons, the experience of war had been grim enough; with them, whole civilizations were at risk. The nuclear age began with the Cold War, some would say simultaneously, for as soon as the United States revealed the unique power at its command, the Soviet Union began to make immediate adjustments to its own behaviour.

The dread of nuclear exchanges provides one explanation for how the world survived such deep superpower antagonism without another total war. Safety,

Winston Churchill remarked in one of his last speeches as prime minister, had become 'the sturdy child of terror'. Few of those responsible for maintaining the peace were content to rely on terror alone. Conventional forces were sustained to ensure that, at the very least, any early clashes between East and West did not lead to an immediate resort to instruments of mass destruction. Because total war was avoided, it is said that deterrence must have worked but perhaps there was nothing much to deter, in that the appetite for war was weak without any added encouragement to abstain or perhaps it was not any particular move made in the name of deterrence but a simple assessment that there were no available military options that could eliminate the risk of utter disaster. This introduces a special difficulty for a military history of the Cold War. It is not really an account of dramatic events, famous victories and humiliating defeats, although these all make their appearance, but must be largely the story of the preparations, intellectual as well as physical, for a war that did not happen.

Of course, this was hardly a time of universal peace. In the name of the Cold War, for example, the United States engaged in two major wars in Asia – Korea in the 1950s and Vietnam in the 1960s and 1970s – while the Soviet Union ruthlessly put down insurrections in its satellite states in Europe and dabbled in a succession of Third World conflicts until it got caught up in a vicious civil war in Afghanistan. During the Cold War period all the old European empires were dismantled. In many cases this involved last-ditch campaigns against local liberation movements: often freedom from colonial rule led almost at once to periods of prolonged instability, with internal violence and border disputes. New states struggled to establish themselves and gain local influence. On occasion this led to regular wars, such as those between Israel and its Arab neighbours and between India and Pakistan. The death throes of colonialism interacted constantly with the ideological and strategic rivalry between the United States and the Soviet Union. If a newly independent state was not inclined to embrace one side in the Cold War, then every effort was made to dissuade it from embracing the other. Poor countries struggling to find their way, often without settled political institutions, found their factional disputes being elevated into critical battles in the struggle to define the future direction of global politics.

Ideological confrontation and the break-up of the old empires produced varying forms of tension and conflict. Neither the Western nor the Eastern alliance was monolithic, and despite the congealed appearance, the external stability often obscured a considerable state of flux. Critical changes took place in economy and society and political philosophy that led to significant variations in attitudes and responses to crises as they developed over the decades of the Cold War. Add to this long-standing cultural and geographical factors and it is not surprising that, though stark in its essence, the struggle took on a complex form.

This short book, therefore, does not even attempt comprehensiveness. This is not the military history of all the conflicts in the period after the Second World War. My focus is on the dominant themes of strategic thinking and military

planning among the major powers over this period. I describe the changing political context and also those important conflicts and crises that changed the way in which the prospect of further wars was approached by the main players of the Cold War. Throughout the Cold War there was a constant debate over, first, whether strategy must concentrate on preventing the outbreak of future hot wars by making their prospect appear so grim that caution and restraint would always prevail; or, second, whether the priority should be to develop a capability to fight efficiently and effectively on traditional lines, so that a decisive result could be obtained at minimum cost if war did come; or, third, whether to leave the business of preventing war to the diplomats. One critical aspect of this debate was the issue of whether all superpower wars were doomed to follow a tragic path to utter nuclear destructiveness, because of the processes of 'escalation', or whether there was a realistic possibility of containing a major war at the conventional level.

The interaction between hypothetical scenarios for 'conventional' and 'nuclear' war shaped thinking about Cold War strategy. It was influenced by evidence from those hot wars that took place around and beyond the edges of the Cold War, and by the expectations derived from forecasts of new weapons technologies. There were attempts, largely unsuccessful, to release nuclear war from its association with instant horror, while views on conventional war moved from presumptions of the dominance of mass to expectations of information-led precision combat. The starting point lay not in the realm of hypothesis but in the harsh reality of the closing months of the Second World War. This left two powerful images: the irresistible force of the Soviet armoured steamroller as it pushed German forces back from the outskirts of Moscow to Berlin, and the atomic bombing of the Japanese cities of Hiroshima and Nagasaki.

Lenin and Stalin look on as equals as heavy artillery from the Moscow garrison trundles through Red Square during the 1947 May Day celebrations. Only a few years after dogged resistance had been necessary to prevent German troops from entering Moscow, Soviet power dominated half of Europe.

CHAPTER ONE

THE ORIGINS OF THE COLD WAR

IN THE SUMMER OF 1945 the victorious Allies met at Potsdam in the heart of defeated Germany to agree the shape of post-war Europe. Behind the 'Big Three' of Clement Attlee, Harry Truman and Josef Stalin, are Admiral William Leahy, Truman's chief of staff, and then Ernest Bevin, James Byrnes and Vyach Molotov, respectively the foreign ministers of Britain, the United States and the Soviet Union.

THE ORIGINS OF THE COLD WAR

THE END OF THE Second World War found the United States at the peak of its power, the dominant player in the world's economy. It had emerged from the years of struggle against Nazi Germany and militarist Japan comparatively unscathed and having acquired considerable influence around the world. How this influence would be used was uncertain. The man who had seen the country through depression and war, Franklin Roosevelt, had died with victory in sight but with his own ideas for a post-war world still rather vague. His successor, Harry Truman, was largely unknown and untested.

Britain had also experienced a sudden change of leadership, although by election rather than death. Clement Attlee, like Truman, had been a shadowy deputy to a great leader, in this case Winston Churchill, and, also like Truman, had a resolve and toughness of his own. But Britain, unlike the United States, was exhausted, its resources stretched, and with a popular demand for a welfare state that the Labour government intended to meet. Also, again unlike the United States, it did not have the option to stay clear of European affairs. It had learned, courtesy of Adolf Hitler, that radical states could not be easily appeased by acceding to their less drastic demands.

The Second World War comes to an end with the centres of Nazi power in Germany reduced to rubble. Here Russian troops carry the red flag on their way to the smouldering ruins of the Reichstag in Berlin.

The third member of the 'Big Three' that had presided over Germany's defeat, the Soviet Union, was also exhausted after three traumatic decades. Yet at the same time it too appeared to be at the peak of its power. There was no question of a change of leader. Josef Stalin was fully in command, able to mobilize the full resources of society to whatever objective he set without any effective domestic opposition. The Soviet model was being applied ruthlessly to the liberated countries of eastern Europe. One form of totalitarianism was being replaced by another. Even in the western part of the continent, still suffering economic and political disarray after the war, communism was a potent political force, a progressive ideology which could be contrasted favourably to a capitalism that was widely judged to have proved itself inadequate in the 1930s. Communists had played notable parts in resistance movements and were powerful presences in post-war Italian and French politics. Their slogans of progress and the philosophy of central planning fitted in with the expectations of the times.

To Stalin these communist movements were an instrument of foreign policy, subordinate to Soviet interests. He was not interested in any independent communist leaders with their own following – the country with which he almost came to blows in the late 1940s was the socialist Yugoslavia, where Tito was credited with leading resistance to the Germans and the Soviet role relegated to second place. Stalin was wary of all potentially contaminated souls: prisoners of war returning from Germany as well as dissident thinkers and any figure, however notionally loyal to him, with any sort of independent following. What the writer Alexander Solzhenitsyn later called the Gulag Archipelago within the Soviet Union, of prisons, labour camps and places of quiet execution, was expanded to accommodate them. With his well-developed sense of paranoia it would have been surprising if Stalin had put any trust in protestations of goodwill by capitalist countries. They were bound to seek to destroy any socialist state; no chances could be taken.

At the Potsdam Conference of July 1945, Truman, Stalin and Attlee came together for the first time (Churchill departed midway through) to agree on the shape of the post-war Europe. Tensions were evident. In many cases the spheres of influence were clear. Germany was to be divided among the victorious powers and kept under an occupation regime, thereby delaying, though not for long, the struggle to shape its future political identity. Poland inevitably presented itself as a particularly difficult case. It had been the invasion of Poland by Hitler in September 1939, in cynical collusion with Stalin, that had drawn Britain and France into war. The Polish government-in-exile had moved to London and expected to return. With his forces now in full occupation, Stalin wanted his own regime put in place. The idea of a Europe that would be free and democratic was becoming at best a partial vision.

The disturbing logic of the developing situation was set out

Having become president of Yugoslavia after leading his partisan forces as they hounded the Germans out of his country, Marshall Josip Broz Tito (1892–1980) had no intention of being dictated to by Stalin. Stalin's attempt to purge him failed, leading to the first major breach in the Soviet empire.

by Winston Churchill in Fulton, Missouri, in March 1946, when he warned of an 'iron curtain' descending across Europe. At the time this was somewhat provocative for many, especially those still hoping for a re-creation of the wartime alliance in a combined effort for a new world order, with the United Nations at its centre. Those from the West in a position to watch the workings of the Stalinist system at close quarters could confirm the danger signs. George Kennan at the American embassy in Moscow attempted to warn of the inner expansionist dynamic of Soviet power by not only writing a long telegram to his superiors in Washington but by publishing it in the journal *Foreign Affairs* under the mysterious pseudonym 'X'.

In August 1947 President Harry Truman announced the doctrine of containment. The immediate cause was the strength of communism in Europe's southern flank, and the inability of Britain, then in a dire economic position, to sustain its traditional Mediterranean responsibilities. As the Republican majority in Congress, and much of the country, was still under the influence of

Here surrounded by his closest advisers at Potsdam, Stalin's strategy at the time was to gain maximum freedom of manoeuvre to impose his will on the countries that he had liberated. Truman's desire to get Soviet support in the war against Japan gave Stalin an opportunity to gain ground in the Far East.

isolationism, Truman felt that to get even a modest commitment to European security he had to 'sell the threat'. The speech avoided direct reference to communism – he spoke instead of 'totalitarianism' – but the sharply ideological tone was brought out in his contrast between 'two alternative ways of life'. The ideological focus meant that this was as much an issue of 'hearts and minds' of the Western populations as of raw military power gathering in the East. The need was to deal with the economic and social conditions in which the communist appeal might prosper.

This was the logic of the Marshall Plan for the economic reconstruction of Europe, named after the American secretary of state. This acknowledgement that there could be only minimal economic recovery without a boost to the German economy alarmed Stalin, who wanted to keep Germany as weak as possible. He was even more alarmed by the apparent use of dollars to gain American influence. This touched on his hold on power. His own underlings believed that access to Western credits would be extremely helpful. Stalin would have none of

LEFT: *Winston Churchill had had to leave Potsdam after a general election defeat. In opposition in March 1946, speaking at Fulton, Missouri, he warned how 'From Stettin in the Baltic to Trieste in the Adriatic, an iron curtain has descended across the continent'.*

ABOVE: *A critical task of Western policy during the early Cold War was to generate economic recovery in Europe. Britain was as much in need of help as any other country, especially after the harsh winter of*

1947. Here Foreign Minister Bevin, with the austere Chancellor of the Exchequer, Stafford Cripps to his right and Harold Wilson, President of the Board of Trade looking on, signs up to the Marshall Plan in 1948.

The division of Europe after
the Second World War
1945–9

western limit of Soviet occupation or
influence mid 1945

occupied by western forces or
pro-western in sympathy

Soviet occupied or control

Soviet zones of Germany and Austria

original members of NATO
4 April 1949

colonial territories

neutral

Norwegian Sea

Arctic Circle

FINLAND

N O R W A Y

S W E D E N

9

8

7
Estonia

7
Latvia

7
Lithuania

North Sea

Edinburgh

Baltic Sea

Copenhagen
DENMARK

2

1

USSR

IRELAND

Dublin

Hamburg

GREAT
BRITAIN

Amsterdam

Berlin

British zone

Warsaw

P O L A N D

London

NETH.

G E R M A N Y

Brussels

BELGIUM

LUX.

10

Prague

Cracow

CZECHOSLOVAKIA
Communist coup February 1948

5

6

Paris

US zone

Stuttgart

Vienna

3
Budapest

4

FRANCE

US zone
AUSTRIA

HUNGARY

Luxembourg
independent 1945
(incorporated into
Germany 1940–45)

SWITZERLAND

Fr. zone

Br. zone

ROMANIA

ATLANTIC
OCEAN

Alsace Lorraine
returned to
France 1945

from Italy
1947–54

YUGOSLAVIA
Yugoslav–Soviet rift 28 June 1948

Bucharest

BULGARIA

Genoa

Adriatic Sea

small border
areas returned
to France 1945

returned to
France 1945

I T A L Y

ANDORRA

Corsica

Rome

ALBANIA

Oporto

Madrid

S P A I N
Franco's Falangist regime isolated

Balearic Is.

Naples

GREECE
Civil war
1946–49

Aegean Sea

PORTUGAL

Lisbon

Sardinia

Sicily

Athens

Gibraltar, Britain

M e d i t e r r a n e a n

Tangier
International
zone

Algiers

Tunis

Crete

Morocco
Spain

S e a

Morocco
France

Algeria
France

Tunisia
France

Malta
Britain

An enthusiastic crowd of onlookers in late 1948 watches a US Army Douglas C54 Skymaster as it ferries in vital supplies during the siege of Berlin. During the course of the airlift, from June 1948 to September 1949 (it continued after the Soviet Union lifted the blockade in May), 2,323,738 tons of food, fuel, machinery and other supplies were delivered.

THE DIVISION OF EUROPE AFTER THE SECOND WORLD WAR

It took time before the western zones of Germany were amalgamated and gained autonomy, and the communists were defeated in the Greek Civil War. The Sovietization of eastern Europe was a steady process, completed with the Czech coup of 1948, and only effectively resisted by Tito, another communist. Austria did not join the ranks of the neutrals until the country was reunited in a 1955 treaty and promised not to confederate with either West or East Germany.

1. from Germany to Poland 1945
2. from Germany to USSR 1945
3. returned to Czechoslovakia from Hungary 1945
4. returned to Romania from Hungary 1945
5. from Hungary to USSR 1945
6. from Romania to USSR 1945
7. to USSR 1940, lost 1941, retaken 1944
8. to USSR 1940, lost 1941–44, returned 1947
9. to USSR 1947
10. Federal Republic of Germany formed Sept. 1949

this. The attempt to draw credit-hungry socialists into the Western economic system sparked his decision to wage all-out ideological war. This in turn polarized European politics and undermined all talk of 'third ways'. Once the communist propaganda machine was mobilized in a campaign against the plan in the rest of Europe, non-communists were obliged to accept that the time had come to take sides.

The past role of Germany in European affairs meant that its future status was hotly contested. The American, British and French sectors were coalescing into a single entity, while East Germany was already following a Stalinist path. The difficulty was Berlin, also divided among the Allies, but stuck in the heart of East Germany. Free movement was possible across the city divide, and the Allies enjoyed rights of access to the city by train and air. Stalin found this Western outpost a provocation. In June 1948 he attempted to lay siege to West Berlin, and its 2.5 million people, by blocking all rail, road and canal traffic. The United States, Britain and France employed all available aircraft to lift vital supplies of fuel and food into Berlin to ensure that the people could survive. Eventually, in

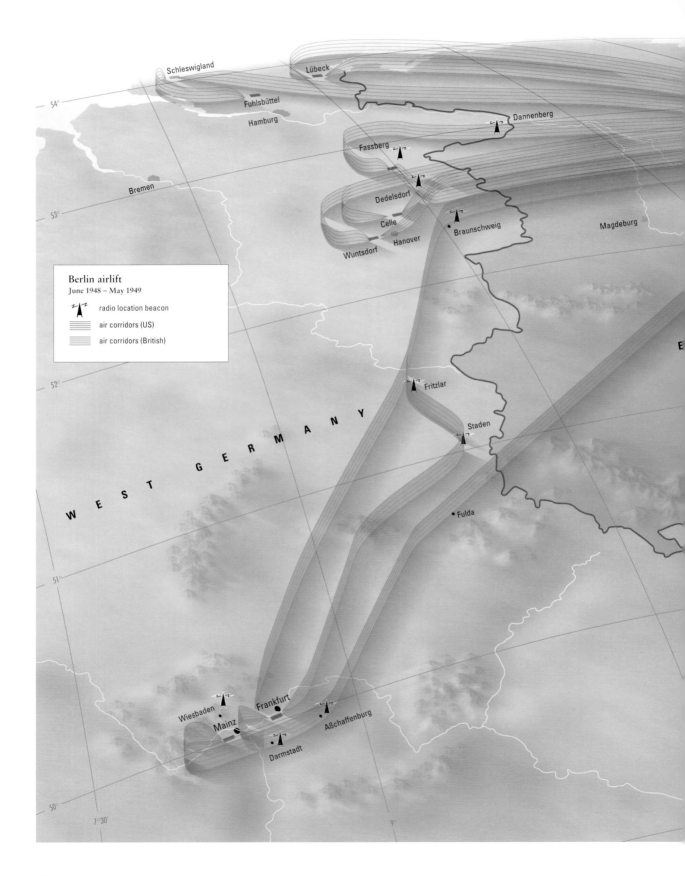

Schleswigland

Lübeck

Fuhlsbüttel

Hamburg

Dannenberg

Bremen

Fassberg

Dedelsdorf

Celle

Braunschweig

Magdeburg

Hanover

Wuntsdorf

Berlin airlift
June 1948 – May 1949

radio location beacon

air corridors (US)

air corridors (British)

WEST GERMANY

Fritzlar

Staden

Fulda

Wiesbaden   Frankfurt

Mainz   Aßchaffenburg

Darmstadt

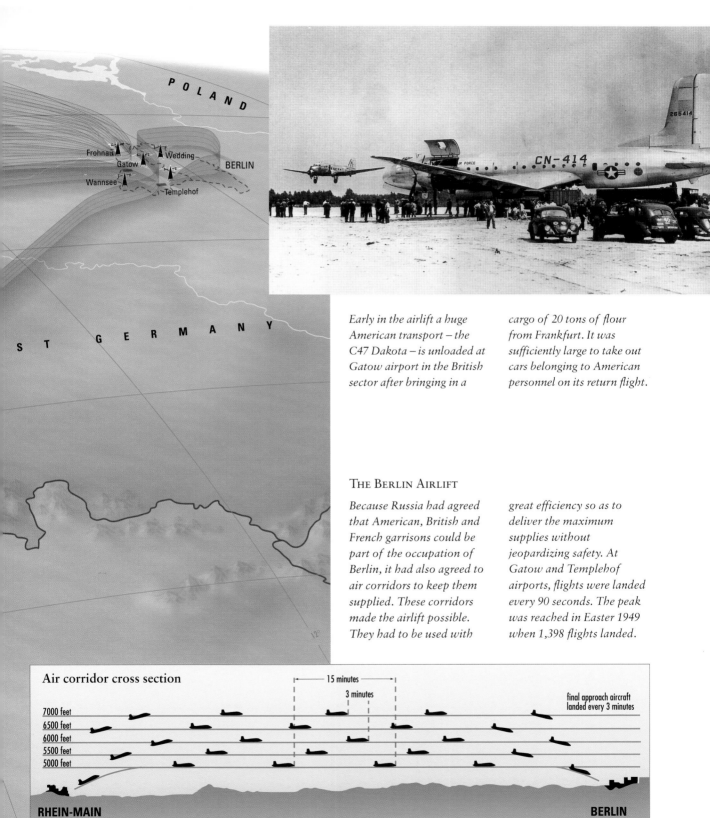

POLAND

Frohnau
Gatow Wedding
Wannsee BERLIN
Templehof

ST GERMANY

265414

CN-414

Early in the airlift a huge American transport – the C47 Dakota – is unloaded at Gatow airport in the British sector after bringing in a cargo of 20 tons of flour from Frankfurt. It was sufficiently large to take out cars belonging to American personnel on its return flight.

THE BERLIN AIRLIFT

Because Russia had agreed that American, British and French garrisons could be part of the occupation of Berlin, it had also agreed to air corridors to keep them supplied. These corridors made the airlift possible. They had to be used with great efficiency so as to deliver the maximum supplies without jeopardizing safety. At Gatow and Templehof airports, flights were landed every 90 seconds. The peak was reached in Easter 1949 when 1,398 flights landed.

Air corridor cross section

15 minutes

3 minutes

final approach aircraft landed every 3 minutes

7000 feet
6500 feet
6000 feet
5500 feet
5000 feet

RHEIN-MAIN

BERLIN

May 1949, Stalin lifted the siege. His ploy had backfired. Berliners began to be seen as doughty victims of communist pressure rather than just former enemies, and policy-makers were put on the alert, prompted to think about how they could prepare the Western world for a communist challenge that seemed to be becoming daily more dangerous.

A communist coup in Prague also provided intense symbolism: it was the failure to prevent German occupation of Czech territory that had exposed the folly of appeasement in the late 1930s. Barely a decade later Western policy-makers did not want to make the same mistake again. Throughout the first decades of the Cold War the memory of Munich haunted Western leaders, urging them to stand up to aggressive dictators early lest they had to defeat them later on. The doctrine was resolute but it was not reckless. What Stalin had he would probably hold, but he must be allowed no more conquests. Soviet power could not be eliminated but could be contained.

Over time containment took the form of a series of alliances with potentially vulnerable states around the periphery of the Soviet bloc. The most important – and durable – of these alliances was the North Atlantic Treaty Organization (NATO). Against the stormy political backdrop of the late 1940s, the United States committed itself to the future security of the European democracies. The instrument of this commitment was the North Atlantic Treaty, signed in April 1949, which contained the critical provision, in Article VI, that 'an armed attack against one or more' of the parties to the treaty would be 'considered an attack against them all'. The comparable Soviet alliance – the Warsaw Pact – was not formed until 1955, ostensibly in response to West German rearmament. However, even by April 1949 a series of bilateral agreements between the Soviet Union and its satellites confirmed their readiness to follow Moscow wherever it might lead, including into war.

It took time before NATO became established as a body prepared to fight a European war under a supreme allied commander. Although American bombers had been moved to Britain during the Berlin airlift, the initial assumption was that Stalin had at this time no more stomach for another large-scale confrontation than did the Allies, and that the possibility of having to fight the United States would be sufficient deterrence in itself. It was only with Korea that the military dimension of the Cold War became fully developed.

EARLY THOUGHTS ABOUT FUTURE WAR

Russia defeated not only Germany but also the German strategic concept. This had sought to avoid the deadly trench warfare of 1914–18 by means of mobility and surprise. The successful blitzkrieg tactics of the first year of the war in Europe combined close air support with tanks to achieve a swift, concentrated attack, throwing the enemy off balance. When Hitler invaded the Soviet Union it was widely expected that he would achieve the same success with the same method. Surprise was achieved and the initial penetration was swift. But Russia was too vast to occupy within days and Hitler's forces became bogged down. The war in the East turned into one of attrition, with German forces often fighting ably but against an apparently inexhaustible enemy defending his home. Gradually the Russians forced the Germans back, with tank battles on a massive scale. By 1945 it was the sheer weight of the Red Army pushing German forces further and further back and eventually taking Berlin that provided a far stronger image than blitzkrieg for those contemplating the course of a future conventional war. Brute force and resilience had been the key to success. This was the logic of the 'permanently operating factors' as adumbrated by Stalin after the battle of Moscow which were to guide Soviet military strategy. It might be added that American military experience, also shaped by the advantage of superior numbers, accepted that some enemies had to be overwhelmed rather than outmanoeuvred. At some point battle had to be engaged and victory would go to the side best able to batter the other into submission.

This had disturbing implications for the western European powers. They had no equivalent response to the Soviet steamroller. The armed forces of Britain and France were stretched by their colonial responsibilities without leaving much spare for Europe. Rehabilitating Germany as a military power was difficult to contemplate so soon after the Second World War, although one indication of the severity of the perceived threat was the speed with which this reached the international agenda. The only real prospect of matching Soviet strength was the United States, but the Americans had rushed to demobilize after 1945 and appeared to be in no mood to rearm, let alone return en masse to Europe. In these circumstances the natural response was to look to the American nuclear monopoly as the best deterrent and, if necessary, active response to Soviet strength on the ground.

AIR POWER AND NUCLEAR DETERRENCE

Prior to the Second World War it had been claimed that air power acting on its own might be a viable alternative to large land armies. This was reflected in the use of the adjective 'strategic' as applied to 'bombardment', suggesting that air raids could be launched over the heads of land forces and thereby send a population into panic and despair, obliging an enemy government to beg for mercy. The experience of the Second World War qualified this optimism. Strategic bombardment did not produce sudden collapses in morale but became another instrument of attrition, at first gradually but then at an increasing pace, eating away at the war-making potential of Germany and Japan. In securing the final victories command of the air had been vital, but it had not been won easily and was not sufficient in itself. The European war was ended by the Allies physically fighting their way into Germany.

The advent of atomic weapons revived thoughts of a decisive strategic instrument. During the late 1930s news came through of a series of advances in nuclear physics that pointed to techniques for splitting the atom and then creating a chain reaction that would unleash vast amounts of energy. War soon provided the incentive to see how far the theory could be taken. After Pearl Harbor, the British effort to design an atomic bomb, which was quite advanced, was merged with the far better resourced American Manhattan Project. Here an international group of scientists, many of them refugees from Nazi Europe, were determined to construct this terrible new weapon before Hitler did. Others hoped that they would perform a service to humanity by demonstrating that it was a practical impossibility. In the event, the weapon was not ready by the time of Germany's defeat in May 1945, and fortunately Hitler's own programme had fizzled out before it was close to success.

The war with Japan was not yet over. Victory was almost certain, but Truman was concerned about the heavy loss of life that would result if an invasion had to be mounted, and was happy to explore all means to get a Japanese surrender as quickly as possible. After the first successful test of an atomic weapon in New Mexico in July 1945, news of which came through as the 'Big Three' assembled at Potsdam, Truman decided to use the couple of weapons available to shock the Japanese government into surrender by demonstrating this terrible power that could now be unleashed. Given the expense of their development he was not inclined to hold the weapons in reserve, and neither he nor his advisers were impressed by anguished pleas from many of the scientists involved that they

The nuclear physicist Robert Oppenheimer and General Leslie Groves, the two leading figures of the Manhattan Project, at the New Mexico site of the first atomic bomb test. Oppenheimer (1904–67), having directed the scientific effort to produce the atom bomb, was never a great supporter of the hydrogen bomb. This, plus his pre-war connections with anti-fascist organizations, led to allegations that he was disloyal and something of a security risk, with the result that his security clearance was lost in 1954.

should either desist altogether or rely on a demonstration shot away from a civilian population. For years both sides had been engaged in air raids of ever-growing intensity, culminating in the fire-bombing of Tokyo the previous March. At this stage of the war the moral argument against attacks on cities had long been lost, provided some military rationale could also be found. The first of the only two nuclear weapons ever to be dropped in anger detonated over the Japanese city of Hiroshima, which Truman described as an important military target, on the morning of 6 August 1945. It led to 200,000 deaths and injuries. The second bomb hit Nagasaki three days later. After another five days Japan surrendered.

The conditions flattered the new weapon. Japan was close to defeat and lacked any means of response. The Soviet Union was also entering the Pacific war. Yet whether or not Japan would have surrendered anyway – as much evidence now suggests – it would also seem that the shock effect of the bombs tilted the internal debate in Japan

LEFT: *'Ground zero' at Alamogordo Bombing Range, New Mexico, twenty-eight hours after the first atomic test on 16 July 1945. This was an implosion device using plutonium-239. Until this time scientists could only guess at the power likely to be released. The explosion released energy equivalent to 21,000 tons of TNT. News of this successful test was immediately transmitted to Potsdam, where Truman felt that his diplomatic hand had been strengthened even though he could only discuss the new weapons cryptically with Stalin.*

RIGHT: *Nagasaki, the second city to be atom-bombed, on 9 August 1945. It had been intended to attack Kokura, but this was covered by cloud, and so the B-29 went instead to the secondary target of Nagasaki. The weapon was of the same sort tested at New Mexico, and with a similar yield of 21 kilotons. About half the city was destroyed and about 70,000 of its people had died by the end of the year.*

towards accepting defeat earlier rather than later. Hiroshima and Nagasaki have been described as the first shots in the Cold War, because they provided an opportunity to demonstrate American strength in a grimly convincing manner to Stalin during a critical stage of the bargaining over the shape of the post-war world. While this may have been a presumed side-benefit, the record shows that

FISSION VERSUS FUSION

Thermonuclear (fusion) weapons represented as important a step change in destructive capacity as had atomic (fission) bombs in 1945. Whereas the yield of atomic bombs was measured in tens of thousands of tons of TNT equivalent and so could be presented as a much more efficient means of achieving comparable effects to the massive air raids of the Second World War, the yield of thermonuclear weapons regularly reached tens of millions of tons of TNT equivalent (megatons).

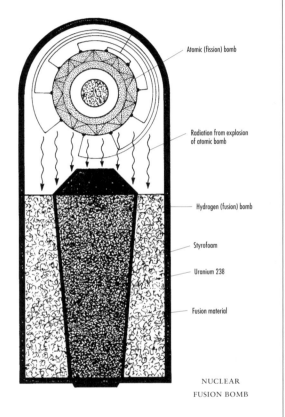

Atomic (fission) bomb

Radiation from explosion of atomic bomb

Hydrogen (fusion) bomb

Styrofoam

Uranium 238

Fusion material

NUCLEAR
FUSION BOMB

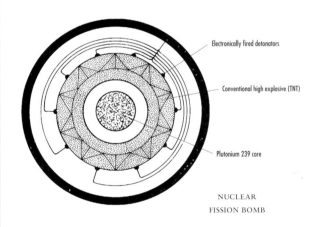

Electronically fired detonators

Conventional high explosive (TNT)

Plutonium 239 core

NUCLEAR
FISSION BOMB

High explosives surround a plutonium sphere. When they are detonated, the plutonium mass is suddenly and drastically squeezed. The mass then becomes critical, and the plutonium begins the fission process, releasing the excess energy in a massive explosion.

In the fusion bomb the explosion of a nuclear fission charge generates energy that fuses deuterium and tritium, releasing neutrons with enough energy to split the (normally stable) nucleus of uranium 238, thus producing an even bigger explosion. This all takes place within less than a millionth of a second.

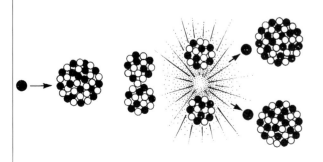

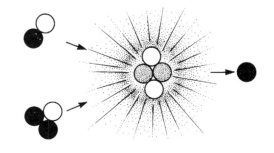

Truman's main concern was with getting the Pacific war over as soon as possible.

The impact of these two attacks on the post-war world was immediate and profound. First they made it possible to imagine circumstances in which Russia could be defeated without having to brave its distances and climate. Second, the association of the new weapons with victory meant that they immediately acquired an aura of decisiveness, whether warranted or not. Third, they confirmed a trend towards progressive barbarism in warfare. Once a major war began there could be no presumption of innocence and no expectation of pity. While at first the stockpile of atomic weapons was very small (indeed, barely more than component parts in the years just after the war), and so appeared as providing merely a more efficient way to mount a conventional air raid, the fact that mass destruction could be instantaneous and include the insidious effects of radiation inevitably led to these weapons soon dominating all speculation on future warfare.

In the first couple of years of peace the Americans took steps to guard their atomic secrets, even from their British allies who had played a significant early role in the weapons development, but they did little to produce many new weapons. That effort began in earnest in 1947, after it had become clear that any hopes for placing this new technology under international control were doomed to disappointment. Proposals had been put forward by the United States, under the name of its chief delegate, Bernard Baruch, to a United Nations committee for the international control of atomic energy. In the circumstances this was a generous gesture, but it could never be convincing to Moscow, which saw in the scheme an early obstruction to its own nuclear programme with a political option whereby the Americans might avoid at a late stage any obligations to relinquish their own arsenal.

It had been assumed by the Americans that the Russians were far behind in nuclear technology. However, by dint of their own hard work, well-placed spies (notably Klaus Fuchs, who had been a British participant in the Manhattan Project) and a full published description by American scientists of their methodology, the Russians made rapid progress. In August 1949 they tested their own nuclear device. As the test came at a time when East–West tensions were growing daily, the effect on the Americans was electrifying. They could no longer assume a nuclear monopoly: they were now engaged in an arms race. The response was not only to step up production of fission (atomic) weapons, but also to press ahead with the next stage of weapons development – the fusion (or thermonuclear or hydrogen) weapon, which promised almost unlimited destructive capacity. Leading American scientists were bitterly opposed to creating 'city-busting' weapons with an explosive yield equivalent to millions of tons (megatons) of TNT, but Truman felt that he had no choice. He dared not let the Russians build such a bomb first.

The president did accept, at the same time, that the Soviet breakthrough required a reappraisal of the strategic role of nuclear weapons. This took the form of a major study, led by the State Department, which considered this new development in the light of the deteriorating international political situation. The other major communist advance in 1949 had been the defeat of the nationalists in the Chinese Civil War. There was now a Sino-Soviet bloc, spreading right through the Eurasian heartland and capable of pushing out against all areas along its periphery. The resulting document for the National Security Council – known as NSC-68 – was designed to bring home to the Washington bureaucracy just how dangerous the situation had become. It warned that without determined action, democracies might succumb to a communist drive for world domination. So long as the United States enjoyed a nuclear monopoly it could be argued that this would serve as a powerful disincentive to Moscow if there was any thought of aggressive action. But if Moscow could retaliate in kind, Western plans to initiate nuclear war would appear reckless. It was therefore unwise to rely on this threat for the indefinite future if it risked bringing a terrible retribution on the United States. The conclusion of NSC-68 was therefore that the remaining years of nuclear superiority should be used to build up conventional forces in Europe capable of coping on their own with a Soviet assault.

KOREA

The proposals in NSC-68 for expensive conventional rearmament initially met with considerable resistance and there implementation would probably have been modest had it not been for events in Asia. The Cold War may have begun in Europe but its militarization came as the result of the Korean War. Until the summer of 1950 Korea had not been high on the list of American foreign policy priorities, but it carried the potential for trouble simply because, like Germany, it had been left divided after the Second World War. Japanese troops to the north of the 38th Parallel surrendered to the Russians and those to the south to the Americans. On this basis two separate states were established as the Cold War took hold and unification talks failed. North Korea (the Democratic People's Republic), led by Kim Il-sung, became communist while the South (the Republic of Korea), led by Syngman Rhee, was as fervently anti-communist. The North received substantial military help from the Soviet Union and was strengthened further when, in 1949, the communists won the Chinese Civil War. Meanwhile the Americans were much more equivocal, largely because of their suspicions of the authoritarian Rhee and concern that he would take precipitate action that could drag them into an unnecessary conflict.

During 1950 tensions between the two sides grew, and then, on 25 June 1950, a surprise attack was launched by the North against the South. South Korean forces, ill-prepared for armoured warfare, buckled under the weight of the North Korean attack. Soon the communist forces had reached the South's capital, Seoul. While Kim had long been pressing for such an attack, which he mistakenly assumed would be backed by a popular uprising in the South, the preparations were orchestrated by Stalin. He had held Kim back until he was reasonably confident that the war would be over quickly and that the Americans would accept defeat (as they had done with China in 1949). Washington was also taken by surprise, and the first question was whether the anti-communist government of Syngman Rhee could be rescued at all. President Truman did not hesitate. He took the view that after China's 'loss', bitterly criticized by his right-wing opponents, Korea's loss would be too great a blow to his foreign policy, and he therefore decided to commit American forces to reversing this aggression.

Helped by the fact that the Soviet Union made a tactical error by boycotting the UN Security Council because of its refusal to recognize China's new regime, the Americans pushed through a resolution demanding that the North Koreans 'withdraw their armed forces to the 38th Parallel' and supporting a UN force to enforce this demand. On this basis Truman announced on 27 June that there would be American intervention. The troops were ostensibly under UN command, and fifteen nations did provide troops in support. However, the supreme commander of the UN forces was General Douglas MacArthur, who had spent the years since 1945 running Japan, and the bulk of the troops supporting the South Koreans were American, suddenly being moved from comparatively relaxed occupation duties in Japan and in a generally run-down state, to hard combat in Korea.

The first task was to establish a foothold. The port of Pusan, to the far south, was established as the entry point. So long as it could be held, supplies and reinforcements could be brought into the country to the point where it would be possible to break out and retake communist-occupied territory. It was soon reached by the North's forces, who pressed hard against it, but American and South Korean forces held, and by this time months of continuous fighting had left the Northern forces depleted. Rather than simply push the communists back, MacArthur conceived of an amphibious operation to land at Inchon, at the waist of Korea, so as to cut off the Northern forces operating in the South from their base. There, on 15 September, American marines landed, supported by naval and air bombardment. A bridgehead was soon established and infantry poured ashore. With UN forces now moving up the country from Pusan, the North Korean Army was soon in disarray and Seoul was back in South Korean hands. Of the 130,000 North Korean troops who had crossed the 38th Parallel, 100,000 failed to return. Now it was North Korean forces that were in rout. General MacArthur was the hero of the hour.

MacArthur pressed strongly for the opportunity to be taken to reunify the country. In principle this was not contested. The dividing line between the two parts of the country was arbitrary: it was not an internationally recognized border. Truman had never assumed that the repulse of the North would be the end of the matter. Though the goal of the military operation had been the liberation of the South the presumption was that this would be followed by a political settlement which would lead to the unification of the country. This was in spite of the fact that the two countries had been sufficiently distinct for the

In April 1951, as the Korean War moves towards stalemate, American 155mm guns fire into distant communist positions north of the 38th Parallel.

KOREA

The ebb and flow of the Korean War. By the time the Americans arrived South Korean forces had almost been pushed out of the peninsula. Then, by November, the tables had been turned dramatically and it was the North Koreans who were pushed back in disarray towards the border with China. Then the Chinese attacked and it was the turn of the United Nations forces to retreat once more before they managed to recover. Eventually a ceasefire line was agreed close to the 38th Parallel, the point at which the conflict started.

United States to declare the North's attack on the South to be aggression. One argument in favour of the UN troops crossing the 38th Parallel into the North was that the UN resolution had required the restoration of international peace and security, and arguably this could not be achieved so long as substantial North Korean forces remained intact, possibly able to mount another invasion. MacArthur's orders were framed in terms of destroying the North's armed forces.

Whether a move into the North was prudent was another matter. So long as the only resistance would come from the North Koreans, then the challenge was straightforward. The real issue was whether the Chinese would be prompted to intervene. There was also a widespread view that the Asian conflict was in essence a decoy for a push against the countries of the newly formed Atlantic alliance in Europe. It had been important to prove to the communists that they could not get away with aggression, but until a substantial rearmament programme, as advocated by NSC-68, had been implemented, Western countries were in no fit state for another total war.

There was a further complicating factor. The communists had only recently taken over mainland China. The defeated nationalist leader, Chiang Kai-shek, had retreated to the island of Formosa (Taiwan) with substantial forces and was anxious to revive the civil war. Most members of the Truman administration saw

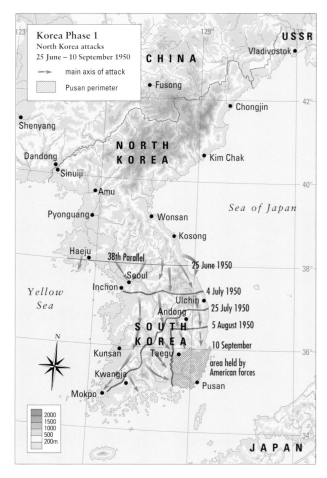

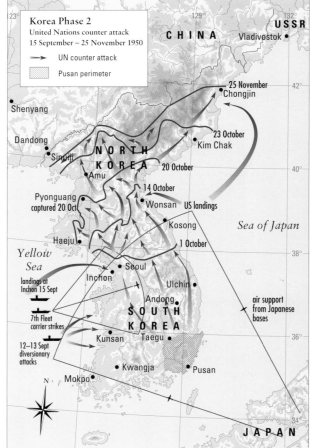

little reason to encourage this: they largely blamed Chiang for his own misfortune. Should the Chinese enter the Korean War then the two conflicts would be much harder to separate. The American right would see this as an opportunity to reverse the result of 1949. In fact, when announcing support for the South Koreans in June 1950, Truman also moved to interpose the Seventh Fleet between Formosa and the mainland, to contain Chiang as much as protect him. MacArthur, however, was of the view that the nationalist Chinese provided a vital resource in the war against Asian communism.

For communist China the possibility that an anti-communist push up from Korea might be co-ordinated with one from Formosa was truly alarming. The Chinese had not been keen on Kim's original invasion and had been kept out of the planning process by Stalin. Their priority was to retake Formosa from the nationalists. As with the Americans and Chiang, Stalin was wary of Mao and was content to have him tied down by Korea. Left on their own, the Chinese began to signal their concern about the course of events, even as the first South Korean troops crossed into the North at the start of October. They could not tolerate an American puppet state on their border. Truman was sufficiently anxious to go to meet MacArthur at Wake Island on 15 October. He asked about the risk of Chinese or Soviet interference. The supreme commander dismissed the

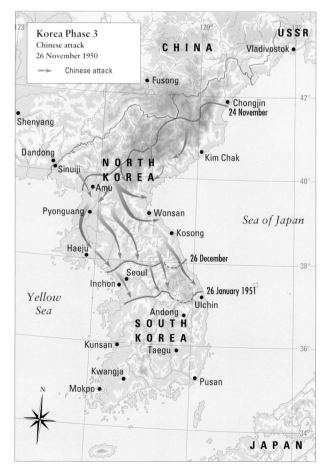

In a bold move American marines landed at Inchon in September 1950, catching the North Koreans by surprise and cutting off supply lines to the North Korean forces. Now under attack from north and south, the army collapsed.

president's concern. He saw very little danger. On MacArthur's count the Chinese had 300,000 men in Manchuria, of which no more than 100,000–125,000 were distributed along the Yalu river, the border with the North. He assumed that barely half of these could get across the Yalu, and that without decent air cover those who did would be slaughtered.

In fact, at this time the Chinese had already begun to infiltrate forces across the river in great secrecy. By 24 October they had completed a deployment of some 200,000 troops, ready and waiting for the UN forces. On that day

MacArthur ordered his generals 'to drive forward toward the north with all speed and with full utilization of their forces'. As they did so their supply lines became attenuated and, equally seriously, the force was split into two parallel armies, unable to reinforce each other. By early November, after there had been a number of skirmishes with Chinese forces, the risk of a wider war was palpably growing, but MacArthur still dismissed this as being unlikely. At most he thought the Chinese would want to save face. To limit the risk he proposed destroying the bridges over the Yalu to prevent the communists getting across. This did not work. The Chinese used pontoon bridges as they continued to add to their forces in North Korea. The numbers were soon well over 300,000, but largely concealed.

On 24 November UN troops reached Hyesanjin, close to the Yalu. The next day China launched a massive counter-attack, with which the UN forces could not cope. Once again an army was in retreat across Korea. There was now in Washington a real fear of a massive defeat of US forces. MacArthur, whose complacency was much to blame for this dire situation, now swung to alarmism. He argued that a war was under way with the entire Chinese nation. He demanded a variety of forms of escalation including drawing in troops from nationalist China and blockading the Chinese coast. On 30 November Truman promised that 'We will take whatever steps are necessary to meet the military situation, just as we always have', and did not deny that this might include the use of atomic bombs. There was some discussion in Washington of the possibility of drawing on the very small stock of atomic weapons then available, but the idea did not get very far because of the international condemnation this would have aroused, and the uncertain military value of any detonations. The British, already alarmed at the thought of being drawn into a war with China, strenuously objected.

Chinese and North Korean troops crossed the 38th Parallel once more and retook Seoul, but in January the UN and South Korean forces rallied and repelled the attack. Seoul was liberated, and soon both sides were facing each other at the war's starting point, the 38th Parallel. Truman appeared ready to negotiate an armistice. MacArthur was not ready for this at all. He took China's reverses as evidence that despite fanatical bravery and 'gross indifference to human loss', China lacked 'the industrial capacity to provide adequately many critical items necessary to the conduct of modern war'. The enemy, he declared,

> must by now be painfully aware that a decision of the United Nations to depart from its tolerant effort to contain the war to the area of Korea, through an expansion of our military operations to its coastal areas and interior bases, would doom Red China to the risk of imminent military collapse.

He proposed to his notional superiors a massive expansion of the war and the direct involvement of the nationalist Chinese. To the Joint Chiefs, getting involved in an even deeper conflict with communist China would be, to quote General Omar Bradley, 'the wrong war at the wrong place at the wrong time and with the wrong enemy'. Truman, now thoroughly alarmed, sacked MacArthur in April, disregarding the political risks of taking on such a popular general. MacArthur's own alarmism about the position of the UN forces was undermined when improved American tactics combined with superior firepower to repulse Chinese and North Korean attacks that were becoming desperately reliant upon 'human wave' tactics.

It took until July, when the Chinese and North Korean forces had been pushed back beyond the 38th Parallel again, for China to accept the offer of ceasefire talks. These began at Panmunjon on 12 November 1951 but it took until

The flight of civilians is a familiar accompaniment to war. Here Koreans, desperate to avoid the fighting, wade through a river carrying their belongings.

27 July 1953 for there to be an actual ceasefire agreement. During the intervening years many died in fierce ground fighting, although there was never again the sort of dramatic advance that had marked the first nine months of the war. It settled down into a dogged contest reminiscent of the First World War, but without the futile offensives. There were continual American air raids, but by the summer of 1952 there were few targets left of any conceivable strategic value. The raids nevertheless continued to exact a heavy toll on North Korean civilians.

One reason why the talks took so long was the refusal of the South to return to the North prisoners who had no wish to go back. When President Eisenhower came to power at the start of 1953, he took the view, with his secretary of state John Foster Dulles, that another reason for intransigence was the self-imposed limitations on the American war effort, of which the most important was the toleration of sanctuaries for communist forces on adjacent Chinese territories and the refusal to use nuclear weapons. Eisenhower and Dulles were convinced that hints on their part that these limitations might be eased were an important reason for the breakthrough. More important, however, was the death of Stalin, for he had been satisfied that the stalemate kept the Americans, and for that matter the Chinese, tied down. Without him Russia could be more pragmatic.

General Douglas MacArthur had immense personal prestige, acquired during the Pacific war. Here it is being added to by President Truman with another decoration. Eventually MacArthur's assertion that there 'is no substitute for victory' and his direct challenge to Truman's more limited approach to the Korean War led in April 1951 to the president relieving him as UN commander and as commander of US forces in the Far East, to be replaced by General Matthew B. Ridgway.

CHAPTER TWO

THE ARMS RACE

DURING THE 1950s no shape symbolized the nuclear age more than the familiar mushroom cloud, here appearing as the result of an American test on a Pacific island.

THE ARMS RACE

MASSIVE RETALIATION AND LIMITED WAR

In their different ways the Truman and Eisenhower administrations believed that their strategies for Korea had been not only appropriate but also a source of guidance for the future. Their differences had little to do with conventional forces which, by and large, were still employed according to the methods of the Second World War. Large conscript armies fought as well as they could, backed by air power in both combat support and attacks on the enemy's socio-economic structures. The differences lay in their assessments of the influence of nuclear weapons.

Although the war became unpopular in the United States, members of the Truman administration believed that they had demonstrated how wars should be fought in the nuclear age. All-out war with nuclear weapons seemed to be just too dangerous. They were proud that nuclear attacks and the extension of the war into Chinese territory had been eschewed while the original objective – the liberation of the South from the North – had been achieved. The conclusion was that there was a need to prepare to fight traditional sorts of war on the assumption that two nuclear arsenals might neutralize each other and that the absolute aim of forcing unconditional surrender from the enemy would be unattainable. The NATO countries, meeting in Lisbon in 1952, agreed to an ambitious build-up of forces that would permit, if necessary, large-scale conventional operations. This programme soon began to impose strains on the Western economies and it became apparent that the targets were unlikely to be met. At the same time the era of nuclear scarcity was starting to come to an end. Conventional divisions, properly equipped, were expensive, but the production lines for nuclear weapons were starting to roll.

The critics of Truman believed that he had been foolish to require the American military to fight in such a restrictive way and to get bogged down in a costly, frustrating and inconclusive war as a result. Furthermore, they saw continued dependence upon conventional warfare as playing to the communists' advantages in both manpower and disregard for human life. Eisenhower, by contrast, decided to abandon the attempt to compete in conventional strength and capitalize instead on the growing nuclear arsenal of the United States. The conviction that hints of nuclear use had helped get the communists to accept the Korean armistice confirmed this inclination. In

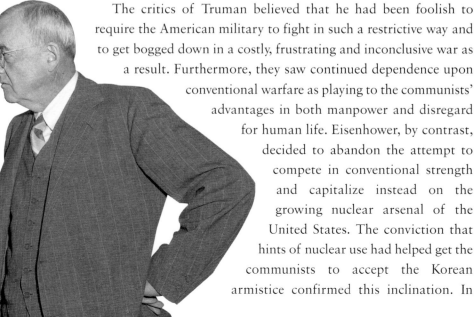

President Dwight D. Eisenhower with his tough secretary of state John Foster Dulles, conferring in September 1953. Dulles (1888–1959) had long been determined to take charge of US foreign policy. He established anti-communist alliances around the Sino-Soviet periphery, founded on NATO, but taking in South-East Asia (SEATO) and later Central Asia (CENTO), involving Turkey, Iraq, Iran and Pakistan.

January 1954 John Foster Dulles announced what became known as the doctrine of Massive Retaliation. Dulles believed that it was neither feasible nor desirable to develop local forces to counter communist aggression at any of the many points where it might occur. He therefore argued the need to 'depend primarily upon a great capacity to retaliate, instantly, by means and at places of our own choosing'. The principle was that so long as the Soviet leaders knew that any war was likely to be total, steps would be taken to avoid provocation; if they were allowed to think a war might be limited, then they might be tempted to try their luck. This might have been no more than a short-term measure to take advantage of American nuclear superiority while it lasted, but Dulles's presentation invited the charge that this was a new and reckless dogma that would be followed after superiority had been lost.

Instead of becoming less dependent on nuclear threats, as Truman had intended, NATO was becoming more dependent. As part of the original attempt to match the Soviet bloc's conventional strength, West Germany had been allowed to rearm. This was the only way a conventional balance was at all feasible. Germany had no intention of joining NATO to provide a battleground, and so required that its territory be defended at the inner-German border. This became known as Forward Defence. Once it was admitted that Germany could not be defended by conventional forces then any move by Soviet bloc forces over the border was likely to invoke nuclear deterrence. Yet when American nuclear superiority was neutralized by the arrival of a comparable Soviet capability the deterrent effect would be lost. Equally dangerous, Moscow might judge American threats to be incredible only to discover that they were meant to be taken seriously, with a nuclear catastrophe the result. To drive home this point, Dulles remarked that it was important to demonstrate a readiness to go 'to the brink' to restrain Soviet expansionism. To his critics this appeared reckless: any East–West crisis might soon escalate because all limited options had been precluded.

The acquisition of equivalent retaliatory power by the Soviet Union would mean that nuclear threats would lose credibility. It might be argued that deterrence did not require a theory of rational action, but a recognition that some situations were so inherently irrational that they could trigger powerful passions and cravings for vengeance or retribution, sufficient to drain concepts of rationality of meaning. If rational decision-making prevailed, then provocations, even the most extreme, might not lead to nuclear retaliation. But who was going to rely on rationality when so much was at stake and the processes of decision-making were liable to be confused and disrupted? Because nuclear war was such a horrendous prospect, even the slightest risk of its initiation could have a deterrent effect.

When pushed, this was the essence of NATO's deterrence thinking: the probability that one side might unleash a nuclear war was small, but given the consequences of miscalculation, even a small probability provided a powerful argument for caution. Yet at moments of relative calm, when the question of how a nation might act in the face of the most severe provocations was posed, it was hard to promise irrationality, let alone sound reasonable when asserting the likelihood of a nuclear offensive following a conventional attack against a third country. The Atlantic alliance sought to deter a communist offensive against the European democracies through an American threat to initiate nuclear war. This was known as Extended Deterrence. Yet once the United States was as vulnerable as everyone else, why should it give such an awesome security guarantee to its allies? If given, should it be believed? Would Washington really be prepared to go to war on behalf of Paris, Bonn and London when Chicago and New York were equally at risk?

The response to this predicament proposed by advocates of limited war was to accept that as all-out war could not be pursued, then neither could all-out objectives. Armed force must be restrained and controlled to serve specific political objectives, to a level proportionate and appropriate to the stakes and circumstances. The corollary of accepting that the West dare not bring the central confrontation with the Soviet bloc to a head was that even when immediate interests had been protected by armed force, the adversary would live to fight another day. This argument had some weight in areas of marginal interest where

THERMAL AND BLAST
EFFECTS OF A 20KT BOMB
IN LONDON

BLAST:
0–1 total destruction;
1–2 massive structures
    destroyed;
2–3 wide-scale destruction;
3–4 high-rise buildings
    badly damaged;
4–5 factories damaged;
5–6 low-rise buildings badly
    damaged;
6–7 vehicles destroyed/
    overturned;
7–8 wooden structures
    destroyed

HEAT:
A   metals vaporize
B   metals melt
C   plastic/rubber ignites
D   wood burns
E   third-degree burns
F   second-degree burns
G   first-degree burns

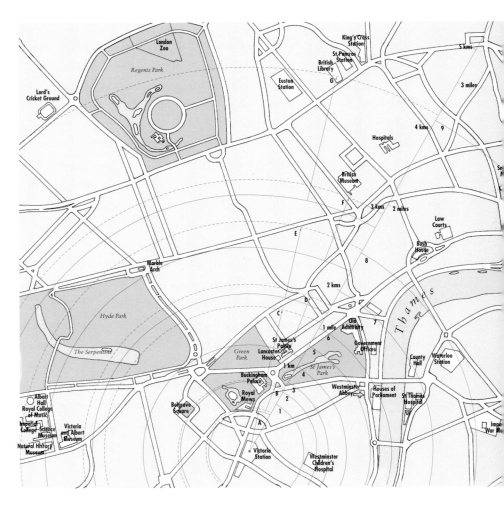

the moderation of objectives was possible, but Europe was a different matter. If a Soviet attack came, there could be no limited objectives for NATO. Either it was repulsed or it prospered. There could be no moderate, compromised outcome. The West German government was particularly concerned by the idea that communist forces might grab a bit of its territory and then accept a ceasefire. With such 'salami tactics', each slice of the salami would not be worth major war, but when all were lost the defeat would be total. The logic of this argument was that there were no halfway houses for NATO: either the threat of a nuclear riposte must be unequivocal or the quality of the conventional defence must be unassailable.

TACTICAL NUCLEAR WEAPONS

One middle way was actively canvassed during the 1950s, and was followed by the US Army: small nuclear weapons for battlefield use, integrated into NATO's general-purpose forces. The associated doctrine derived from the distinction, developed with conventional air power, between the 'tactical' and the 'strategic', according to which the former was geared to influencing the course of combat on the ground and the latter sought to achieve a decisive political result

independently of ground combat. Limited-war theorists agreed that it was foolish to rely on the decisive effect of strategic nuclear weapons, given the development of an equally 'decisive' Soviet capability. However, one group, for whom Henry Kissinger was an influential, albeit temporary, advocate, argued that tactical nuclear weapons could be used effectively to prevent the Soviet Union achieving its military objectives on land. His critics argued that a 'limited nuclear war' was a contradiction in terms.

Although initially tactical nuclear weapons represented an area of Western superiority, once the Soviet Union caught up with strategic weapons this advantage would inevitably pass. It was still hoped that somehow these weapons would favour the defence, in that an attacking force would need to concentrate and in doing so would provide rewarding targets for such devastating explosives. Nuclear munitions employed in this way would be little more than efficient forms of conventional firepower and so should not be subject to the same inhibitions as the larger nuclear weapons. 'No different from a bullet', Eisenhower at one point seemed to say. However, it soon became apparent that these weapons could also help the offence, in the manner of traditional artillery, by blasting a way through defences. Moreover, it was illusory to suppose that they could be used as if they were essentially conventional. Exercises in the mid 1950s indicated that if nuclear weapons were exploded on a substantial scale, but only by NATO, enormous casualties would be caused among the population supposedly being defended. By the end of the 1950s those who wished to avoid early recourse to strategic nuclear war, including Kissinger, had accepted that this required being prepared to fight for some time with conventional forces. If tactical nuclear weapons had a role, it was to reinforce the deterrent by making it even harder to stifle escalatory pressures. Basing nuclear weapons in Europe was also taken to be a demonstration of the American commitment to European security. What they could not do was provide a means of escaping from the impossible choice between an unaffordable conventional defence and an incredible nuclear deterrent.

PREPARING FOR NUCLEAR WAR

Another possible escape route would have been to find a plausible way to fight a nuclear war. This became harder rather than easier with the growth of the nuclear stockpiles. So long as the numbers were small, nuclear use would result in catastrophe but not necessarily a condition from which recovery was impossible. Even up to the late 1950s Soviet leaders were suggesting that the vast size of its territory and dispersal of its population gave it a strategic advantage vis-à-vis the United States in any nuclear exchange. Soon, however, they were reminding the Chinese that nuclear weapons do not 'obey the class principle'. Chinese leader Mao Tse-tung was said to have observed that even if 300,000 Chinese were killed, there would be another 300,000 ready to continue the fight. In his memoirs Khrushchev recalled a conversation with Mao by the side of a swimming pool, in which he warned that 'with the atomic bomb, the number of troops on each side makes practically no difference to the alignment of real power and to the outcome of a war. The more troops on a side, the more bomb fodder.'

Equally important for Moscow was the reduced relevance of distance. The routes into Russia were well trodden, but invaders had always been thwarted, albeit at great cost. Long-range bombers and missiles could, however, leap over Russia's vast hinterlands. During the 1950s a network of Western air bases began to be established close to the Soviet borders from which nuclear bombs and then medium-range missiles might be delivered. Soviet leaders began to complain of encirclement. Soon it was clear that even eliminating those hostile bases could not eliminate the threat. Long-range ballistic missiles could deliver a lethal punch in minutes over many miles. It was hard to see how this punch could be resisted.

The trends were, if anything, more disturbing for the Americans. It was many years since they had had reason to worry about a land invasion. The Japanese attack on Pearl Harbor in 1941 had been an awful shock because of the loss of so much of the fleet, rather than because it was a precursor to an assault against the

West Coast. At any rate, by the end of the war, with its economy booming and its cities untouched by enemy bombardment, the United States had good reason to feel secure. In the late 1940s there were concerns about atom bombs being floated into ports by visiting merchant ships or carried through customs in suitcases, but by and large there was confidence not only in American superiority but also in the difficulty the Russians would face in delivering the weapons.

Missiles would be the answer. Towards the end of the Second World War, London faced subsonic V-1s (the first cruise missiles), against which forms of defence could be devised. Against the ballistic V-2 missile, built by Wernher von Braun and his team (who later carried on their work for the US Army), little could be done. The threat remained until the launch sites were overrun by Allied troops. After the war both superpowers experimented with cruise and ballistic missiles, but the speed and relatively greater accuracy of the ballistic missile had the advantage. (An early American test cruise missile famously hit the wrong continent, ending up in the Amazon rainforest.) Until it saw the lead being taken by the Soviet Union in missile development and production, the US Air Force remained committed to the long-range bomber as the most efficient means of delivering nuclear bombs. The Russians had begun to put together an intercontinental bomber force but they did not persevere, preferring to concentrate on a missile force and, with the US Air Force fixated on bombers, they chalked up some impressive firsts. The summer of 1957 saw the first successful test of an intercontinental ballistic missile (ICBM). There followed an even more dramatic achievement, at least in terms of propaganda, that October: the launch of the world's first artificial earth satellite, Sputnik 1. American opinion was stunned. This meant that in critical respects American technology could not be considered superior to that of the Soviet Union, and apparently in one vital capability was inferior. Even worse, as Sputnik emitted its beeps passing over the United States, there could be no doubting the vulnerability of the American homeland.

For the rest of the 1950s, encouraged by exaggerated claims from Soviet leader Nikita Khrushchev and some worst-case analysis from the US Air Force, there were regular claims that the Soviet Union was racing ahead in ICBM production so that a 'missile gap' was developing that would leave the United States too weak to cope with Soviet threats. Those urging a crash US effort in all

One of the most controversial figures of the American missile programme was Wernher von Braun (1912–77), here sitting in a mission control room. A pioneer in rocket science, he had made his name masterminding the German V-1 and V-2 programmes during the Second World War.

The first earth satellite, Sputnik 1, was a source of immediate fascination. Orbits taking it over San Francisco and New York made clear the strategic implications behind the scientific achievement. This British newspaper image points to the moment when it would pass over London.

areas of high technology warned of the consequences of inferiority. 'What would the Americans find if they reached the moon?' a scientist was asked during congressional hearings. 'The Russians!' he replied.

President Eisenhower did his best to rebut these claims. A top-secret spy plane, the U-2, was making regular flights over Soviet territory and had failed to find any hard evidence that missiles were being deployed on any scale. The fact that the United States had been caught out by Sputnik, and that its own missiles had an unhappy record of failure at the testing stage, did not help his credibility. (I recall a playground ditty to the tune of Perry Como's 'Catch a Falling Star': 'Catch a falling Sputnik, put it in a matchbox, send it to the USA.') Then, in May 1960, a U-2 was shot down by Soviet air defences. The Russians waited for the American denials that they had been engaged in espionage before revealing that they had captured both the plane and its pilot, Gary Powers, intact. The result was not only a major international embarrassment for Eisenhower, but also a loss of critical intelligence. In fact, although few recognized this at the time, the Americans were already starting to pull ahead in the missile race. Their own programme was back on schedule and the production lines were rolling.

Taken around 1952, this picture shows a prototype of the Boeing B-52 Stratofortress bomber. Through different models, the B-52 became the workhorse of the US Air Force. Although designed to carry nuclear bombs, it gained notoriety during the conventional air raids over Vietnam in the 1960s and 1970s and then again over Iraq in 1991. There are plans to keep it in service until well into the twenty-first century.

On 1 May 1960 an American U-2 spy plane that had flown over Russian territory from a base in Turkey was shot down by a Soviet surface-to-air missile. The American cover story, that this was a meteorological aircraft that had strayed off course, was blown away when the Russians were able to display both the wreckage and the pilot, Gary Powers.

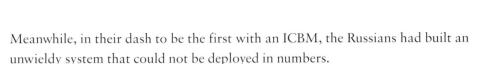

OPPOSITE: *The mushroom cloud is just forming minutes after a nuclear explosion at the American testing ground at Nevada, watched by American civilian defence officials and reporters some 10 miles away.*

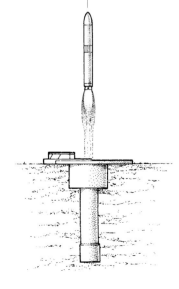

Meanwhile, in their dash to be the first with an ICBM, the Russians had built an unwieldy system that could not be deployed in numbers.

The critical requirement in any nuclear victory would be the ability to hit the enemy's missiles and bombers before they had been launched, thereby imposing disarmament. Then, instead of being locked in an indefinite stalemate, aware that nothing could be done to prevent a devastating attack on one's own society once nuclear exchanges began, it might just be possible to knock the enemy out of the game, leaving him helpless in the face of an overwhelming superiority. The capacity to execute such an attack was described as a *first-strike capability*; the capacity to absorb such an attack and still be in a position to retaliate, a *second-strike capability*. A first strike would be the most demanding task ever to face a military planner. As large a proportion as possible of the enemy's means of retaliation would have to be destroyed on the ground and then any bombers or missiles that escaped would have to be intercepted before they reached their targets. There would be no margin of error. Thus the planner would need to be confident that *all* the necessary targets had been identified and shown to be vulnerable; that sufficient weapons of the right kind were available to attack them; and that the attack could be co-ordinated effectively to hit all the targets virtually simultaneously, even over a wide geographic area. If the attack was staggered then there would be a risk of the first detonations prompting an immediate riposte by the enemy. If insufficient enemy systems were destroyed then the defence might be overwhelmed by a full retaliation. There would always be a risk that missiles would be launched as soon as the first signs of an impending attack came through on the radar screens. Even preparing for such an attack could provide the enemy with warning.

The danger in all of this was not simply that one side might strain to acquire a first-strike capability and fail, but that fear that the other side had made the critical breakthrough, or, worse still, was about to attempt to execute a first strike, would lead the potential victim to strike out in anticipation. At times of crisis, with nerves already on edge, one side's moves being misinterpreted by the

BALLISTIC MISSILES

There were three possible means of protecting missiles from being caught in a surprise first strike and the Americans considered all

three for its Minuteman ICBM programme. The first, as indicated by the name, was to launch on warning, the second was to move around,

and the third was to ride out an attack in reinforced concrete silos. The third of these was preferred as the safest option.

other could have catastrophic consequences. If the early-warning radars mistakenly signalled incoming missiles, and the operators failed to check lest, as happened on occasion, it was something as innocent as a flock of geese, then real missiles might be launched.

Could the United States and the Soviet Union confront each other with massive nuclear arsenals on hair triggers through a succession of crises without something terrible happening? The British author C. P. Snow declared it to be a statistical inevitability that the catastrophe would come during the 1960s. As it turned out, this was far too pessimistic. The leaders of the superpowers might feel obliged to sound tough, if only for the sake of deterrence, but the nuclear age made them cautious and caused them to seek to avoid getting

I'LL STOP MY TESTS IF YOU STOP YOURS I'LL STOP MY TESTS IF YOU STOP YOURS I'LL STOP MY TESTS IF YOU STOP YOURS I'LL STOP MY TESTS IF ...

By 1957 all three established nuclear powers were becoming aware of the harmful effects of the radioactive fallout generated by regular atmospheric nuclear tests but, as this 1957 cartoon by Vicky shows, none were prepared to make the first move.

panicked into desperate measures. By the start of the 1960s, ideas were circulating for direct links between the Kremlin and the White House to ease communication, avoiding those types of weaponry that might scare the other side into thinking that a first strike was imminent or else trigger vicious cycles of moves and counter-moves.

The drive to find some way of regulating the nuclear age was further reinforced by popular discontent with the harmful environmental consequences of nuclear testing in the atmosphere. The first serious attempt to get a US–Soviet agreement on nuclear matters began in 1958 with talks on a nuclear test ban. Initially they did not get very far because of concerns over how compliance with such a ban could be monitored. American scientists opposed to a ban suggested the Russians might dig deep caverns in hard rock to avoid a test being detected, and they also warned that without testing they could not develop the weapons systems necessary for American superiority.

Having started the nuclear age in such a confident fashion, the Americans were finding its complexities and hazards difficult to handle. At one level the two sides shared an interest in a stable strategic balance. Every effort had to be made to avoid war through miscalculation. At another level the United States dared not

allow the Soviet Union to get a usable superiority and so had to make the development of its own second-strike capability a high priority, largely by putting missiles on submarines, which were far less likely to be detected than fixed land bases. At yet another level the Americans really needed a first-strike capability if the foreign policy commitments that they had made to allies were to be credible. Deterrence depended on being ready to use nuclear weapons first. The more the Soviet Union could develop a second-strike capability, the more foolish first nuclear use appeared and the less credible deterrence.

THE NEW NUCLEAR STRATEGY

So challenging were all these issues that during the 1950s a whole new breed of civilian strategist came into existence. Many were concentrated at the archetypal think-tank, the RAND Corporation at Santa Monica in California, established by the US Air Force. Nuclear scientists who had cut their teeth during the Manhattan Project had long been providing civilian advice, often opposing military plans for more and better weapons and urging restraint. Now they were joined by social scientists and engineers employing the most advanced methodologies, such as game theory and systems analysis, in order to develop

In July 1959 Vice-President Richard Nixon was showing the Soviet leader Nikita Khrushchev round a futuristic General Electric kitchen of an American model house in Moscow, when they got involved in a fierce ideological debate, known as the 'kitchen debate'. Khrushchev, who understood the threat that American consumerism posed to communist claims to be providing a good life, insisted that the Soviet Union would match the economic performance of the United States.

policies for nuclear strategy and arms control. Albert Wohlstetter led a group that was responsible for the development of the basic conceptual framework of first and second strikes. Tom Schelling demonstrated the dangers of a mutual fear of surprise attack engulfing the two superpowers during a crisis, but also how new strategies might be devised that became competitions in risk-taking, so that one side by edging forward towards the nuclear abyss almost dared the other to move closer still. Herman Kahn, a larger than life figure who was the model for Stanley Kubrick's Dr Strangelove, took Schelling's ideas even further, as he sought

The film director Stanley Kubrick had become fascinated by the bizarre world of the RAND-based nuclear strategists and decided to satirize them in his film Dr Strangelove. *Here Peter Sellers, who played a number of parts in the film, expounds his monstrous ideas as the deformed, German-born Strangelove.*

to show that even once nuclear exchanges had begun, there were ways of conducting operations that might keep the pressure on the other side while avoiding Armageddon.

In general the civilian strategists were more successful in developing ways for stabilizing the nuclear balance than for fighting a nuclear war. They could show what a competition in risk-taking might look like, with early strikes being geared more to making political points than to gaining military advantage, but such 'demonstration shots' were unlikely to appeal to the military and there could be no guarantee that they would be interpreted by the opponent as intended. Did a shot that failed to do much damage demonstrate resolve or an innate caution? In practice, deterrence was unlikely to be boosted because of some ingenious new strategy promising notional victory or at least a wrong-footed enemy. It would be more likely to work because once two superpowers were locked in conflict it was hard to be confident that at some point nuclear weapons would not be detonated. The risk that the irrational passions of war would displace rational calculation provided the best argument for a cautious foreign policy and avoiding unnecessary provocation. It was impossible to prove to Moscow that conventional aggression against the Western alliance would inevitably lead to a nuclear response, but quite easy to show that it just might.

Some argued that a regime led by dogmatic communists, presiding over a country that had shown that it could recover from a loss of 20 million people, might well ignore such risks. Against this, the best explanation for much of Soviet foreign policy was that the experience of 1941–5 had been so searing that Khrushchev and his colleagues were determined that they should never be caught out again. Certainly Sputnik and the missile programme emboldened the Soviet leader, leading him to exaggerate Soviet strength in ways that backfired badly, but he gave no impression that he was trying to create the conditions for a general communist offensive. Rather he focused on two questions. First, how could West Germany be kept in check, so that it did not acquire nuclear weapons, press forward with its demands to reunify with the East and set itself up for what he assumed to be the inevitable next step of another move against Russia? Second, could his country's growing prestige and strength be used to attract the many Third World countries gaining independence from the decaying European empires into the communist bloc?

At the start of the 1960s these two questions led to major crises that produced some of the most dangerous moments in the Cold War but in the end produced a more stable superpower relationship. This was because they helped consolidate the status quo while clarifying the limits of nuclear strategy and the role of deterrence. The first crisis was over Berlin and the second over Cuba. Managing them on the American side was a young and comparatively inexperienced president who took office in January 1961 promising to 'pay any price, bear any burden, meet any hardship, support any friend, oppose any foe, to ensure the survival and success of liberty' – John Fitzgerald Kennedy.

CHAPTER THREE

CRISIS MANAGEMENT

DURING THE EARLY DAYS of the Berlin Wall in August 1961, before it had been built up into a proper wall, West Berliners try to communicate with relatives and friends in the East while a guard looks on. At first the wall involved only barbed wire and cinder blocks. Concrete walls, up to 15 feet high, followed. The eventual system, including electrified fences, watchtowers and gun emplacements, extended 28 miles through Berlin and a further 75 miles around West Berlin.

CRISIS MANAGEMENT

BERLIN

During the 1950s West Germany enjoyed a remarkable economic revival and began the process of rehabilitation, encouraged by its new Western partners to rearm and play a full role in the alliance. By contrast East Germany failed to prosper under communism, while the Soviet Union remained determined to keep it under firm control. These diverging fortunes led the East German regime to regret even more that Stalin had failed to squeeze the Western Allies out of Berlin in 1948. Berlin provided an ideal location for NATO to run spies and work to subvert the socialist system. Most awkward of all, West Berlin was turned into a showcase for capitalism. Because of the open nature of the city, East Germans seeking to escape from the dead hand of state socialism could seek refuge in West Berlin and then get out to West Germany. Increasing numbers took this route until by 1961 there was something of a flood, to over 15,000 a month.

For NATO Berlin demonstrated that, given a choice, people would choose the Western way of life. The effort that had been made to keep it free during the airlift had given it also a special symbolic significance in the Cold War. But its location deep behind the Iron Curtain posed a real problem as it was virtually indefensible. It combined ideological weakness for the East with military weakness for the West. There was therefore every reason to suppose that at some point Khrushchev would seek a military fix to his ideological problem, although he probably always relied more on scaring the Western powers into concessions than on a direct operation to seize the city or cut it off. His first serious attempt to extract concessions came in 1958 when, flushed with the success of Sputnik, he issued an ultimatum. Either the Western garrisons would leave Berlin in return for a new special but poorly defined status or else he would sign a separate peace treaty with the East German government and allow it to handle Berlin as it saw fit. Eisenhower refused to budge and eventually the ultimatum was dropped.

When Kennedy came to office Khrushchev decided that the time was ripe for a revived campaign over Berlin. Partly this was because of the continued haemorrhage of people from East to West. Khrushchev also judged Kennedy to be weak and likely to succumb to pressure. In June 1961, when Kennedy and Khrushchev met for a summit in Vienna, the Soviet leader made his move, attempting to bully the young American president. With another Berlin ultimatum issued, the two leaders departed agreeing on little other than that it was going to be a cold winter.

The two months after the summit were extremely tense. Kennedy summoned his advisers to work out a response. They were divided. One group, led by Truman's former secretary of state, Dean Acheson, took Khrushchev at his word and warned that unless Kennedy authorized a rapid build-up of American strength and demonstrated a steely resolve, then there was no hope of deterring a

Soviet move that would leave Berlin cut off and the Western alliance in disarray. An alternative view was that there was an element of bluff in Khrushchev's stance. By all means take military steps, but at the same time, it was argued, an imaginative diplomacy might help head off a crisis. Khrushchev might settle for something less than his maximum demands.

Kennedy was inclined to offer negotiations, but he soon discovered that giving them substance would not be easy. Any position had to be agreed with Britain and France, the two other Western occupying powers, and Germany. Britain's prime minister, Harold Macmillan, had been through two wars fighting the Germans and now, disinclined to get into another one on their behalf, he was eager for a grand negotiation with Moscow. Such views led the Germans to fear that their aspirations would be neglected in the search for a deal – a deal that would be restrictive and demoralizing without buying off the Russians, who would just keep on pressing until they got exactly what they wanted. Here they were supported by the French president, Charles de Gaulle. He did not expect a war, so believed that a major negotiating effort was unnecessary. In these circumstances he saw a good opportunity to forge a close relationship with the German chancellor, Konrad Adenauer, whose relationships with both Kennedy and Macmillan were poor, as they were irritated by his persistent demands for reassurance that Germany was not about to be abandoned. Adenauer saw a new association with France as a boon not only because it gave him an opportunity to transcend past enmity but also because of the extra freedom of manoeuvre he believed that it would give him in his dealings with Washington.

Kennedy wanted negotiation to solve the problem once and for all. If that was impossible, making the effort would at least show the American people that they were not being asked to accept the burdens of rearmament and the dangers of war without diplomatic options being pursued. He did not see this as an alternative to rearmament but as a complement. Whether the Russians and East Germans were really inclined to move to cut off air, train and road access to West Berlin, this was less likely to happen if he gave a robust response to the ultimatum. When, on 25 July 1961, Kennedy announced his policy, the overall tone was tough. He explained how he could not 'permit the communists to drive us out of Berlin, either gradually or by force'. To emphasize the seriousness of the situation, he urged a national fallout shelter programme to provide some civil defence in the event of a nuclear war.

When Christian Democrat Konrad Adenauer (1876–1967) was first nominated to be chancellor of the new West German Republic in 1949, and this picture was taken, he was already 73. He stayed in power until 1963 dominating German politics. His great success was in overseeing German integration back into mainstream Western politics, including a rapprochement with France, and to secure Allied support for his uncompromising anti-communism.

Diplomatically, what was most significant was not a promise of negotiations – in presentational terms that was par for the course – but the specific reference to *West* Berlin in this speech. As far as Kennedy was concerned, while the United States was in principle committed to maintaining Allied rights throughout the whole city, his special responsibility was to the West Berliners. To Khrushchev this looked like a lifeline. His bluff had failed. Not only had Kennedy's nerve held but he appeared to have fallen under the influence of the hard-line militarists within the Pentagon. Moscow could no longer rely on its terms being met. At the same time, the air of crisis had fed through to East Germany, prompting even more people to flee for the West. Unless there was decisive action soon, East Germany might collapse. Khrushchev therefore decided to implement a plan to separate the

In August 1962, just after the first anniversary of the wall's construction, an 18-year-old East Berlin builder, Peter Fechter, was shot by East German guards as he tried to escape across the wall to the West. People in the West watched helplessly as he lay bleeding to death on the edge of freedom, before his body was carried away by the guards. Over the years about 5,000 East Germans managed to cross the wall while about the same number were captured as they tried and 191 more were killed in the attempt.

two sectors of the city, effectively locking the East Germans in. On the night of 13 August barbed wire went up and cross-border communications were blocked. As it became apparent that there was not going to be a strong reaction from the West, the barbed-wire fence was quickly replaced by a wall, a scar running the length of the city that became the most striking symbol of the Cold War.

In retrospect it is clear that, by dealing with the immediate problem of the gradual depopulation of East Germany, the wall helped bring some stability to the Cold War. That was not how it appeared at the time. The West had been caught by surprise. In part this was because Western strategists had assumed that such a construction was too difficult even to contemplate; in part it was also because they already thought of Berlin as divided, just as the rest of Europe was

BERLIN

The jagged line marks the division of Berlin by the wall. The line had to follow the borders of the Soviet sector, cutting road and rail links and often passing through the middle of streets, requiring the doors and windows of many tall apartment blocks to be sealed. By the 1980s what had developed into a system of walls, electrified fences and fortifications extended through the city. It continued around West Berlin, separating it from the rest of Germany.

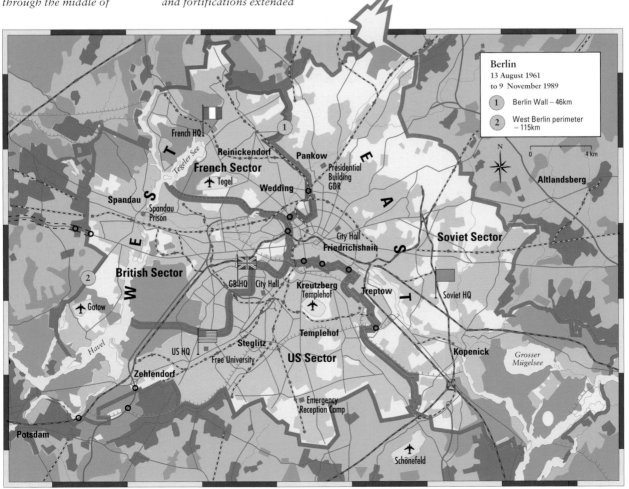

In November 1961 the fortifications separating East from West Berlin are completed in front of the Brandenburg Gate, at the western end of the avenue Unter den Linden. The gate had only recently been restored after war damage. As long as the wall was in place the gate was shut off to both East and West Germans.

divided. The reality of the wall was something different. The West Berliners felt vulnerable and forgotten. To reassure them Kennedy sent his vice-president to the city, where he met troops that had been sent from West Germany up the autobahn. The air of tension continued, and in September Checkpoint Charlie, a crossing-point between the two parts of Berlin, gained notoriety as American and Russian tanks faced each other across the border. Yet soon Khrushchev had eased the ultimatum, ostensibly because of diplomatic progress, but more because he realized that his forces were in no state to take on the West.

This point was driven home by the Kennedy administration in October 1961 when a speech by a Pentagon official revealed that the latest intelligence demonstrated that if there was a 'missile gap' it now favoured the United States. New intelligence had come in from the first reconnaissance satellites and from a high-ranking agent, Oleg Penkovsky, in both cases revealing the difficulties faced by the Russians when it came to deploying ICBMs. Khrushchev found his assertion that the United States and the Soviet Union were equal as super-powers in every respect undermined, and a dangerous vulnerability revealed that might be exploited in a future conflict. He tried to obscure this weakness through bluster and a new test series that culminated in a monster detonation of 56 megatons, the largest explosion ever. For someone who believed that raw military power was vital to successful diplomacy, this was not the time to go to the brink. Yet to back down indefinitely on Berlin would represent a humiliation

In June 1963 in one of the most famous speeches of his presidency, with his back to the Berlin Wall, the city's mayor (and later German chancellor), Willy Brandt, at his far left and a large and enthusiastic crowd in front of him, John Kennedy proclaims 'Ich bin ein Berliner'. The reception was so rapturous that Kennedy later observed that those in the crowd might have tried to tear down the wall with their hands if he had encouraged them to do so.

that he could not contemplate. Perhaps emboldened by their military strength, the Western countries were offering very little of interest in negotiations. Khrushchev hectored Kennedy in a private correspondence but got only polite rebuffs in return. Unless he could do something to restore the Soviet military position, then the prospect for Moscow was gloomy. Over time missile numbers could be built up. But Khrushchev was impatient. He wanted a quick fix.

When Khrushchev decided in April 1962 that he should send missiles to Cuba, it was in part because this seemed to be an easy way of closing the gap with the Americans in short order. If he could put medium-range missiles, of which the Soviet Union had ample stocks, some 90 miles from the American mainland, they would become, in effect, ICBMs. He may well have hoped that when the new missile bases were ready and he could reveal them to the world, this would give him a springboard for yet another Berlin initiative.

THE BAY OF PIGS

It is probably also the case that the missiles were sent for the reason claimed at the time: to defend Cuba against an American invasion. Cuba was the latest and in many ways the most significant recruit to the socialist cause. Fidel Castro had started not as a communist but as one of the more determined opponents of the dictator President Fulgencio Batista. He fought a guerrilla war against an increasingly demoralized army that effectively collapsed at the end of 1958. Once in power Castro set himself on a collision course with the American government by nationalizing US-owned oil refineries and other assets, and also questioning the status of the US naval base at Guantánamo. President Eisenhower responded by putting an economic squeeze on Cuba and also by resorting to one of the traditional methods of dealing with radical regimes in Latin America, that is, seeking to destabilize them by covert means. By the time that Kennedy took over from Eisenhower in January 1961 diplomatic relations had been broken and Moscow was already taking a close interest in this unexpected development. There were close to Castro some communists who wanted Cuba to join the socialist camp. Castro himself was wary but he felt that if his country was not to be brought to its knees by American economic pressure there was nowhere else to go. The more he moved in this direction, and appeared ready to embark on a campaign of subversion throughout the Americas, the more Washington was determined to topple his regime.

Kennedy inherited a plan devised by the Central Intelligence Agency (CIA) to use Cubans disillusioned with Castro's undemocratic behaviour and his move to socialism to mount an invasion. They had been gathered at a training base in Guatemala, and the idea was to mount an amphibious operation with air support to land the force. This was a high risk plan, and the presumption of those involved was that if the going got tough then Kennedy would authorize the intervention of American forces. Kennedy had no intention of doing any such thing and tried to make this clear. During the election campaign he had committed himself to support the Cuban rebels, and he would not want to be accused of abandoning them. He had also a romantic view of guerrilla warfare. This flowed from his conviction, prevalent at the time, that the Cold War had moved into the Third World and that the West must find new policies and strategies to compete with the communists. Part of his response was reflected in the Alliance for Progress, an initiative to encourage an economic revival in Latin America to reduce the political opportunities that another Castro might exploit. The other part was to encourage anti-communists to adopt guerrilla techniques to fight the communists on their own terms.

Against this background he preferred that the rebels aimed to get inland and beat Castro at his own game. The CIA humoured him, explaining that it would

January 1959 and 33-year-old Fidel Castro, surrounded by his guerrilla fighters and supporters, addresses a rally in Havana after the former dictator Fulgencio Batista had fled. Initially some in the United States urged that he should be welcomed as a reformer after years of repression and corruption, but his socialist policies soon infuriated Washington.

be impossible to put small numbers of guerrillas into Cuba but promising that if the rebel brigade failed to stimulate a general uprising or got into trouble then a guerrilla campaign could still follow. They maintained this position even when Kennedy's demand for a quieter landing spot led to the choice of the Bay of Pigs as the landing site, quite unsuitable for any guerrilla campaign. This was typical of the lax and naïve planning, with the cover story flimsy and the training inappropriate. There was a contradiction between the requirements of landing 1,400 men, including the need for air support, and the requirement that this be done with stealth, and then the requirement for stealth with the noise necessary to spark an uprising in Cuba. A number of advisers saw a disaster in the making but their doubts were weakly expressed and insufficient in the face of the

momentum behind the project. Apart from anything else there was uncertainty as to what to do with the rebels, camped in Guatemala, if they did not go to Cuba. In the end the planners still seemed to assume, despite the president's explicit instructions, that American forces would retrieve the most disastrous operation.

The result was a humiliating fiasco in April 1961 leaving the rebels killed or captured when they landed at the Bay of Pigs. The first, pre-invasion air attacks had a moderate impact and they were abandoned when the cover story that these were dissident Cuban pilots became incredible. The landings were chaotic, with many ships caught by the puny Cuban Air Force and those forces that did get ashore soon overwhelmed by superior Cuban units. Kennedy was put under intense pressure to bail out the operation, by mounting air strikes, but he refused, despite the enormous blow to his prestige that the failure involved. He acknowledged that this would simply make a bad situation even worse.

An American-backed attempt by 1,400 Cuban rebels to overthrow Castro's regime in April 1961 collapsed in farce. This was neither a proper invasion, backed by airpower, that the CIA had envisaged, nor the guerrilla landing that Kennedy wanted. Here Cuban artillery pounds away at hapless rebels on the beachhead.

On 24 October 1962, in the face of doubts (notably in Britain) about the veracity of American claims that Soviet missiles were in Cuba, President Kennedy ordered the release of reconnaissance photos, such as this one of a medium-range missile base, with explanatory captions.

CHERRY PICKER

LAUNCH PAD WITH ERECTOR

LAUNCH PAD WITH ERECTOR

MISSILE READY BLDGS

CABLING

OXIDIZER VEHICLES

FUELING VEHICLES

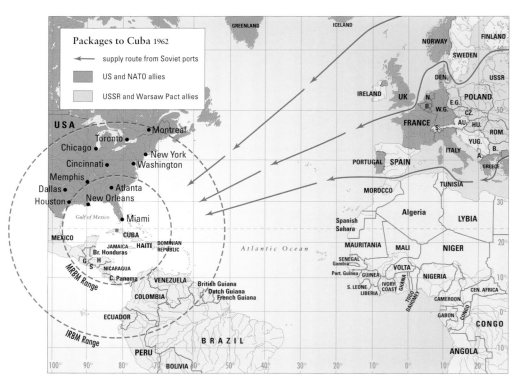

Packages to Cuba 1962

→ supply route from Soviet ports

US and NATO allies

USSR and Warsaw Pact allies

The Cuban missile crisis

Although the missile crisis was about nuclear weapons its outcome was shaped by the overwhelming local conventional advantages of the United States. Cuba was far from Soviet shores and only supplied with difficulty, despite the fact that it was less than 100 miles from Florida. It even reluctantly hosted an American naval base at Guantánamo Bay.

Mounting a blockade posed no military problems for the Americans, nor did air strikes or invasion. Kennedy's concern was not only that any offensive action might trigger a nuclear riposte, but also that his forces might get bogged down in the face of Cuban resistance and that Khrushchev might retaliate against West Berlin.

THE CUBAN MISSILE CRISIS

This left Kennedy cautious when faced with advocacy of future military adventures but still fuming about Castro, who followed the Bay of Pigs by rounding up his opponents and declaring Cuba a socialist state and himself a lifelong Marxist–Leninist. Kennedy approved a covert programme, known as Operation Mongoose, designed to encourage opposition to Castro, but this made little impact. This, plus preparations for an overt intervention, was sufficient to lead Castro to ask for increased military support from the Soviet Union. Khrushchev took the opportunity to get Castro's permission to establish missile bases in Cuba. Castro, who was ready to accept missiles as an act of socialist solidarity but did not believe them necessary to defend Cuba, wanted this to be an open deployment; Khrushchev preferred that it be covert. If Castro had won this argument Kennedy would have been badly placed to object because American missile bases were strung around the periphery of the Soviet Union. As it was, Kennedy was furious to discover the deception after members of his government had been playing down the importance of Soviet support to Cuba.

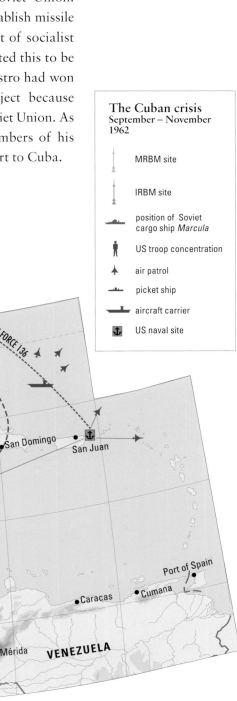

The Cuban crisis
September – November 1962

- MRBM site
- IRBM site
- position of Soviet cargo ship *Marcula*
- US troop concentration
- air patrol
- picket ship
- aircraft carrier
- US naval site

On 14 October 1962 pictures of Cuba were taken by a U-2 reconnaissance aircraft. Analysis the next day revealed signs of the Soviet missile bases under construction in the Caribbean island. The next morning Kennedy began to discuss with his advisers an appropriate response. After a week of intensive deliberation a policy was agreed based on a limited quarantine of shipments of military hardware to Cuba, against a backdrop of preparations for major hostilities. American strategic nuclear forces were placed on alert. The alternative would have been to mount an immediate air strike to destroy the missile bases. Although initially tempted, Kennedy rejected this step because it would have looked like American bullying, was not guaranteed to succeed in destroying the bases before some operational missiles were fired, and seemed to lead inevitably to a full-scale American invasion of the island and possibly Soviet retaliation against Berlin. The quarantine put pressure on Khrushchev without humiliating him, and appeared prudent to other nations. The quarantine allowed time for a diplomatic solution, but the president was well aware that if Moscow refused to remove the missiles then he would be under enormous pressure to return to the alternative.

The policy was announced by the president in a televised speech on 22 October. Over the next few days channels of communication were opened up to the Soviet Union to explore a possible settlement. Initially these produced little response, and although some Soviet ships held back, reluctant to break the quarantine, there was no sign of any readiness to remove the missiles. On 26 October a letter from Khrushchev indicated the outlines of a possible settlement, with withdrawal of the missiles in return for an American promise not to invade Cuba, but this message was contradicted by an apparently more official statement from the Soviet leadership the next day which called for an explicit link between these missiles and American missiles in Turkey. Also on that day, 27 October, a U-2 flight was shot down over Cuba.

Kennedy and his advisers decided to respond to the first of the Soviet letters and not the second. That evening Robert Kennedy, the president's brother and closest confidant as well as the attorney general, delivered a message to the Soviet ambassador, Anatoly Dobrynin, offering assurances that there would be no invasion of Cuba, and at the same time providing an unofficial promise that the missiles in Turkey would be removed and an unofficial warning that matters were reaching a head. The next day Khrushchev, by now extremely worried that matters were getting out of control, accepted Kennedy's terms, and the crisis was effectively over.

There was a collective sigh of relief at this point that nuclear war had been avoided. This was the most high-profile crisis of the nuclear age, with the two superpowers in direct confrontation over a nuclear issue. Many of those involved on the American side were fearful that the inability of either side to back down would lead the two into a chain of events that would end with catastrophe. Khrushchev wrote how the 'smell of burning' hung in the air. Yet while the crisis demonstrated the need for good intelligence and diplomatic imagination in crisis management, in many ways it was one of the more manageable. The issues were clear-cut, the urgency was evident, and the ability of third parties, including Castro, to influence the outcome was limited. If Kennedy had decided to act against Cuba there was little that Khrushchev could have done about it as the balance of power in the Caribbean overwhelmingly favoured the United States. If Khrushchev had decided to lay siege to West Berlin in retaliation, then Kennedy would have sought to break the siege by means short of nuclear war.

None the less, one reason for the anxiety was a growing awareness that even in the starkest of crises the leaders of the two superpowers could lose control of the situation and find themselves obliged to act in perilous ways. The shooting down of an American U-2 was one example of this; another U-2 on an unconnected mission straying into Soviet territory was another. The way that the US bomber force went on alert or the standard procedures adopted by the US Navy for mounting a blockade could lead to inadvertent encounters that could catch policy-makers unawares as they plotted their next moves in the belief that they were engaged in something more akin to a game of skill and intelligence than one of chance.

After the crisis, Khrushchev accepted that there were limits to his ability to conduct the Cold War through threats and ultimatums. The missile crisis was followed by an immediate deterioration in relations with the other great communist giant, China. Relations had been uneasy for some time because Mao

Kennedy and Khrushchev greet each other warmly at the start of the June 1961 Vienna summit. When they departed, relations between the two were much more frosty as the Soviet leader handed over an ultimatum over Berlin and Kennedy warned of a 'cold winter' to come.

found it difficult to take Khrushchev seriously as the true inheritor of Stalin and the leader of the international communist movement, and because he was furious that he was given so little support in his own drive to build up a Chinese nuclear arsenal and to pursue his campaign to reunify China by pushing the nationalists out of Taiwan. Moscow tried to be conciliatory but Khrushchev was not going to risk war for the sake of China, and once he realized that any moderation was going to be damned by Beijing as a sell-out to imperialism, he decided that he might at least get the benefits of détente by putting relations with Washington on a more constructive level. The main fruit of this détente was the partial test ban, signed in August 1963. While the problems of verification, and Russia's reluctance to have any on-site inspection of its facilities, still got in the way of a comprehensive treaty, a partial ban at least had the advantage of eliminating the sort of testing that had become deeply unpopular as a symbol of the nuclear age, and a feared form of atmospheric pollution.

CONVENTIONAL STRATEGY

Robert McNamara, the ultra-energetic secretary of defense who served Presidents Kennedy and Johnson, was determined to raise the nuclear threshold – that is, the point where NATO would be forced to make the terrible choice between nuclear release and surrender. He did not accept that improving conventional forces would dilute the nuclear deterrent: he could not see how any threat that was too dangerous to implement could serve as a credible deterrent.

The response from America's allies was unenthusiastic. A conventional strategy would be comparatively much more expensive. In addition, the allies argued, if past commitments meant anything, extended deterrence should work because in strategic terms Europe was as vital to Washington as was the continental United States. If McNamara accepted that an attack on the American homeland might warrant nuclear retaliation, then why not an attack on Europe? The Europeans were also nervous about the idea of deterring only nuclear war and the inference that conventional war, especially if it could be confined to Europe, was tolerable. Nuclear war was uniquely terrible, but conventional war would be terrible enough, especially for those countries providing the battlefields. They pointed to the risk that if the Soviet Union did not deem its own country to be at risk in a future war, because conventional fighting would be confined to the continent's centre, then it might be much more tempted to indulge in exploratory aggression.

There seemed to be no point in trying to match the conventional strength of the Warsaw Pact. One reason for this was the distance of the United States from its European allies. Since the early 1950s all intelligence estimates had pointed to many more Warsaw Pact divisions than NATO ones. The normal figure cited was 175 as against 20. There was a sense of hopelessness in the military balance that made any attempt to close the gap appear futile. As the Allies doubted whether the Russians were that keen on a major war in the best of circumstances, and assumed that Khrushchev would not dare discount the possibility of nuclear use, deterrence was probably working fine. Kennedy was prepared to increase the size of the US Army force based in Europe, but once fighting had begun it would take many days to ship extra forces across the Atlantic, with the constant risk of being caught by Soviet submarines en route. Against this the contiguity of the Soviet Union with its allies meant that the Red Army should have no problem in getting reserves to the front.

McNamara was unconvinced. On his staff were some of the brightest analysts from RAND whom he had brought in to ensure that established assumptions and positions were all subjected to the most professional scrutiny. They began to investigate the conventional military balance in some detail. They soon discovered that many of the Warsaw Pact divisions were under strength and that, when a careful analysis was undertaken, the gap between the two sides shrank dramatically to the point where a determined effort by the Allies could close it. The analysis was helped by Khrushchev's own assumption that there was not much point in devoting too much money to large armies that would not survive long in conditions of total war. He had announced reductions in Soviet conventional forces in 1960, and these had only been partly reversed during the Berlin crisis.

As Secretary of Defense from 1961 to 1967 Robert McNamara was one of the most formidable figures in both the Kennedy and Johnson administrations. Here he gives testimony to a congressional committee in August 1963 in favour of an atmospheric test ban, arguing that the United States was comfortably superior to the Soviet Union in nuclear power.

The analysis left the Allies unimpressed. They suspected, unfairly, that McNamara produced figures to suit his own policy predilections. Even if his figures were correct, that still left the argument that any increase in forces involved an unnecessary expense and undermined confidence in nuclear deterrence. Kennedy himself soon lost interest in this debate. By 1963, after the Cuban missile crisis, and with Berlin relatively quiet, he judged a European war unlikely. The cost of American troops in Europe in terms of foreign exchange was bothering him, and as the Allies were not going to improve their capabilities he was loath to make an exceptional American effort when, in the end, it was European security that was at stake. By this time he was also finding his allies, especially Adenauer and de Gaulle, irritating.

FRANCE'S DISSENT

Charles de Gaulle had not enjoyed having to play second fiddle to Britain and the United States during the Second World War and he enjoyed it even less during the Cold War. He took power in France in 1958, with the country reeling from a succession of foreign policy defeats: the failure to hold on to Indo-China after being defeated by the Vietnamese communists at Dien Bien Phu in 1954; the débâcle two years later when a joint effort with Britain and Israel to topple President Nasser of Egypt following his nationalization of the Suez Canal had to be abandoned in the face of US pressure; and the continuing and vicious conflict to sustain French rule in Algeria. A French nuclear programme was already under way and de Gaulle saw this as a way to rebuild French independence and self-confidence.

American proposals for flexible response went wholly against this project. An alternative Gaullist doctrine was developed based on the proposition that the most credible form of deterrence involved a virtually automatic nuclear riposte in response to an unambiguous and mortal threat to the state. Not only did this argue against reliance on non-nuclear threats, but it also warned against relying on allies, especially when they were an ocean away, who could not be expected to see threats in the same light. Once third parties were involved nuclear automaticity became incredible. France was challenging not just a greater role for conventional forces at the early stages of a conflict but the whole idea of alliance in the nuclear age.

France sought to appeal to its European partners, encouraging them to act independently of the Americans (a category for which de Gaulle's purposes included the British). As we have seen, initially West Germany was tempted, for Adenauer saw the French card as a way of putting pressure on the Americans to be more supportive of the German position, including the eventual reunification of his country. But the French doctrine, with its presumption of national selfishness, gave France's allies no reason to suppose that the French would be more reliable than the Americans, and they would be a lot less powerful. Germany was at the front line of the Cold War yet could not follow the Gaullist route, for it had forsworn nuclear weapons on being allowed to rearm in the 1950s. It was dependent upon other nuclear powers extending deterrence. The offer to put Germany, and the rest of Western Europe, under its nuclear umbrella had been made by the United States at a time when it enjoyed superiority. Even when superiority was lost, the offer was sustained because the situation in Europe had stabilized and Washington accepted that to withdraw nuclear protection from Germany would be unnecessarily disruptive to good alliance relations. The British also developed their own nuclear forces, but they always insisted that their nuclear forces were supplemental to those of the United States and not an alternative. They even became dependent upon the United States to stay in the nuclear business after their own long-range missile programme was abandoned. In December 1962 President Kennedy agreed to sell Polaris submarine-launched missiles to Prime Minister Macmillan, thereby allowing Britain to stay in the nuclear business, but at the same time confirming de Gaulle's distrust of the Anglo-Saxon 'special relationship'. With Germany and Britain both sticking with the United States, France became more isolated. In 1966 de Gaulle announced that France was to leave NATO's integrated military command, while remaining a member of the alliance at the purely political level.

France's departure made possible the formal adoption by the rest of the alliance of flexible response. The practice was now some distance from McNamara's original concept. The Allies agreed but without any commitment of extra forces, while the Americans themselves, by now bogged down in Vietnam, were unable to offer much themselves. Meanwhile, the Russians, having begun the decade running down their conventional forces, had now entered a period of expansion and so the gap in conventional capabilities was, if anything, widening. The basic change was that rather than move straight to nuclear retaliation, NATO would at least attempt to hold back any Warsaw Pact offensive in the hope that time could be bought for a diplomatic initiative to restore stability. If that failed the likely next step would be the use of *tactical* nuclear weapons before the last resort of *strategic* nuclear use.

MUTUAL ASSURED DESTRUCTION

In 1961 the other part of McNamara's plan for reducing the risk of all-out war was to find a way of controlling the course of nuclear hostilities once they had begun. In the spring of 1962 McNamara announced to NATO at its Athens summit that henceforth the United States would prepare to fight a nuclear war as if it was a traditional military operation – that is, by attacking military targets first and going for cities only as a last resort. It was described as the 'no-cities' doctrine.

McNamara probably accepted this proposal as a means of providing one possible way of squaring the circle of America's nuclear guarantee to its allies with his belief that the threat to use nuclear weapons lacked credibility. It appeared to offer the opportunity, if war had broken out, of postponing the most terrible devastation and so buying some time to find a way out of the conflict. This would require both sides to play the same game, and it was hard to believe that calm reason could survive any nuclear use. The Russians were soon mocking the idea of 'Marquis of Queensberry' rules for nuclear war. They saw a much more sinister implication.

The idea had been developed during the years when it was assumed that the missile gap

The initial rationale for MIRVs (multiple independently-targeted re-entry vehicles) was that they would allow strategic forces to cover many more targets with the same number of missiles. It was then realized that they would have advantages in swamping ballistic missile defences. The nose cone of this Minuteman III missile, safely in a silo and enclosed by a sealed concrete hatch, contained three warheads.

MIRV

In mounting a nuclear attack, multiple warheads would not only overwhelm defences but also ensure that a wide range of targets, including missile and bomber bases, were hit. Submarine-launched missiles were more likely to catch the enemy by surprise and, by attacking its decision-making structure, might paralyse it and so prevent the orders for retaliation being issued. This was, however, a thin reed upon which to rely, as there was always a risk of the enemy launching on warning of an incoming attack and of alert bombers or missiles at sea escaping the best executed strike.

would favour Moscow but was now being outlined at a time when the gap was growing in favour of the United States, with new Minuteman ICBMs and Polaris submarine-launched ballistic missiles being introduced at an impressive rate. If the Americans really could hit missile bases and other military targets, then why wait until they were empty after their contents had been launched against the United States? It was thus hard to distinguish the no-cities doctrine from a first-strike capability that might just tempt a reckless leader into launching a disarming surprise attack. In fact, some American policy-makers had investigated this option during the Berlin crisis. They concluded that the first-strike option existed, but that it was very dependent upon the quality of its execution and, while it might substantially reduce the risk of retaliation against the American people, it could do little to spare Europe from Moscow's vengeance. In addition the whole idea of launching such a strike out of the blue also seemed repugnant.

McNamara was personally sceptical about any idea that nuclear weapons could be used for war-fighting. He later wrote how 'In long private conversations with successive presidents – Kennedy and Johnson – I recommended, without qualification, that they never initiate, under any circumstances, the use of nuclear weapons.' In October 1962 Kennedy, shocked by the Cuban missile crisis, was

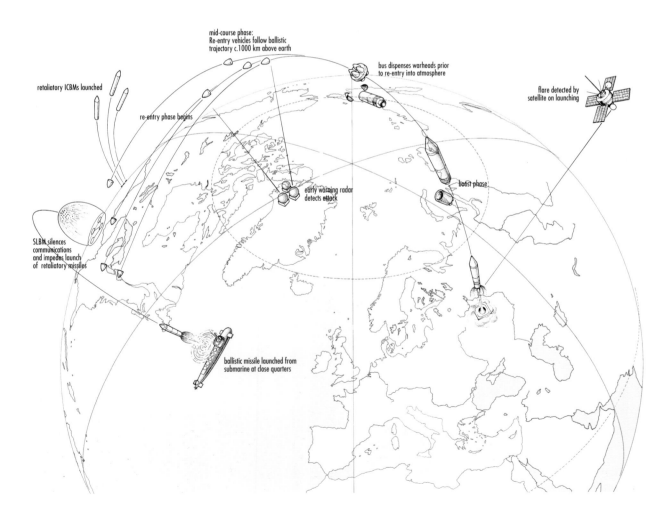

mid-course phase:
Re-entry vehicles follow ballistic trajectory c.1000 km above earth

bus dispenses warheads prior to re-entry into atmosphere

flare detected by satellite on launching

retaliatory ICBMs launched

re-entry phase begins

early warning radar detects attack

boost phase

SLBM silences communications and impedes launch of retaliatory missiles

ballistic missile launched from submarine at close quarters

determined to reduce even further the role of nuclear weapons in American foreign policy. This was reflected in his drive for the partial test-ban treaty. He had toyed with the thought that, if a war began, then a first strike might make some sort of sense, but had become steadily convinced that such escalation would just guarantee catastrophe. McNamara certainly had little interest in a first-strike option and he could not but note the vehemence of the Soviet response when he went public with the new doctrine in a speech at Ann Arbor that July, and also the extent to which the US Air Force did seem to have an interest in first strikes, and was using the new doctrine to justify provocative new programmes.

By the end of 1962 the doctrine had disappeared from view. Soon it was replaced with a much more stark doctrine: *assured destruction*. The position now was that so long as the United States had a secure second-strike capability,

SUBMARINE-LAUNCHED BALLISTIC MISSILES

Carrying missiles on submarines was an obvious way of protecting them from a surprise attack, as submarines generally stayed ahead of anti-submarine warfare techniques, although the idea met with resistance from airmen who *believed that delivering nuclear weapons was their responsibility and the surface admirals who believed that this was a distraction from the navy's main business. The method of launch, shown here with an early Polaris test* *from the USS* Henry Clay, *was 'cold'. Missiles were ejected from tubes within the submarine to the ocean surface by compressed gas before the rocket engines were ignited.*

described as the ability to destroy the Soviet Union as a twentieth-century power even after absorbing a surprise first strike, then deterrence was intact. As McNamara had no intention of authorizing an American first strike, he professed himself content if the Soviet Union took steps to reassure itself about its second-strike capability, for example by building submarine-launched missiles. He could see the danger of an unstable situation in which either side felt that it would be worse off if it did not take the initiative. A condition in which both sides had secure

Nuclear Standoff
1970

USA and allied states

USSR and allied states

US missile base

Soviet missile base

US naval base

Soviet naval base

US bomber base

Soviet bomber base

second-strike capabilities was described as Mutual Assured Destruction. This had the unfortunate acronym MAD, which was seized upon by McNamara's critics as if some profound point was being made. In practice the term was more descriptive than prescriptive. Both sides could assure the destruction of the other, and that provided good reason for caution at times of crisis.

McNamara used this doctrine to argue against the deployment of anti-ballistic missile (ABM) systems. It was this that generated such hostility from his critics. Superficially it seemed hard to argue against the proposition that everything possible should be done to protect the American people against a missile attack. The trouble was that defence against missile attack was (and still is) very difficult. The defender has to have a comprehensive coverage and be constantly on the alert. The attacker, probably at far less expense, could add extra weapons, or even decoys, thereby complicating the defence so that the defender might have to waste scarce interceptors on irrelevant targets. This point was emphasized through the development of multiple independently targeted re-entry vehicles (MIRVs), which increased the number of individual warheads per launcher. A vast collection of incoming warheads accompanied by a variety of decoys promised to swamp any conceivable defence.

Initially the Russians shared the view of McNamara's opponents that it was perverse to put a brake on ABM deployment. The doctrine of assured destruction seemed to turn morality upside down. Offence was good: defence was bad. Killing cities was good: killing weapons was bad. In a famous encounter, Soviet premier Alexei Kosygin, attending a 1967 summit with President Johnson, berated McNamara for suggesting that defences should be stopped. At the time ballistic missile defences were being constructed around Moscow. As far as Kosygin was concerned it was the duty of any government to take all steps to protect its people, a view shared by many of McNamara's opponents in the United States, who had been lobbying insistently for a major American deployment. As news of MIRVs leaked out of Washington during early 1968, the Soviet leadership took the point and hesitated in the construction of the defences around Moscow.

By this time President Johnson, fearing that McNamara's stubbornness on this issue was handing an electoral advantage to the

NUCLEAR STAND-OFF

By 1970 the nuclear relationship between the USA and the USSR had come to be described as one of mutual assured destruction. This map helps illustrate why. With missile bases scattered around their countries, and each base containing many weapons spaced out so that single warheads could not expect to knock out more than one missile, plus naval bases managing large numbers of missile-carrying submarines, a successful first strike would have been an enormous undertaking that would almost certainly have failed to prevent a retaliatory attack.

Republicans, instructed McNamara in September 1967 to go ahead with an American deployment. However, as a barely convincing compromise, and to avoid a new round of the arms race, this was presented as a precautionary deployment against a possible Chinese ICBM capability that might emerge in the early 1970s. It gained some credibility because the Chinese were not only in an intensely militant mood, but had also moved swiftly from testing their first atomic bomb in October 1964 to their first thermonuclear weapon in June 1967. McNamara's announcement, one of his last as secretary of defense, was mainly notable for his warnings against allowing the development of a technological offence–defence race between the superpowers.

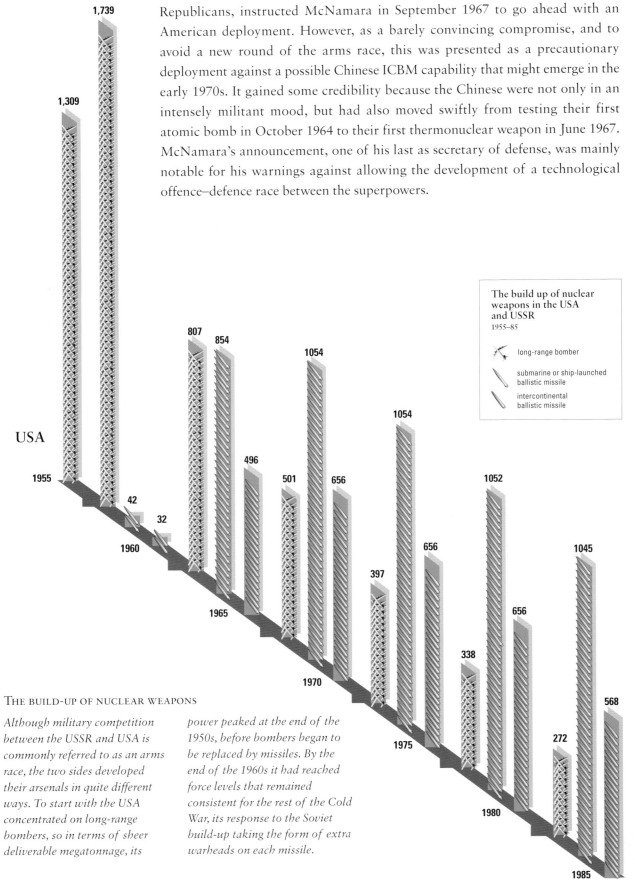

The build up of nuclear weapons in the USA and USSR
1955–85

✈ long-range bomber

submarine or ship-launched ballistic missile

intercontinental ballistic missile

THE BUILD-UP OF NUCLEAR WEAPONS

Although military competition between the USSR and USA is commonly referred to as an arms race, the two sides developed their arsenals in quite different ways. To start with the USA concentrated on long-range bombers, so in terms of sheer deliverable megatonnage, its

power peaked at the end of the 1950s, before bombers began to be replaced by missiles. By the end of the 1960s it had reached force levels that remained consistent for the rest of the Cold War, its response to the Soviet build-up taking the form of extra warheads on each missile.

Sobered by evidence of new American weaponry, underlining McNamara's warning, Moscow moved during 1968 to accept President Johnson's January 1967 offer of talks on limiting strategic arms. The Soviet-led invasion of Czechoslovakia thwarted any early start to the talks, and it was left to Richard Nixon to preside over the negotiations from 1969 to 1972. Vietnam had left the American people weary of the effort and expenditure associated with the Cold War, and détente with Moscow was politically popular. So it suited Nixon effectively to start his 1972 election campaign in Moscow, signing a treaty limiting ABMs and imposing interim restrictions on offensive weapons. By this time strategic developments had already conspired to produce a degree of stability in the nuclear balance.

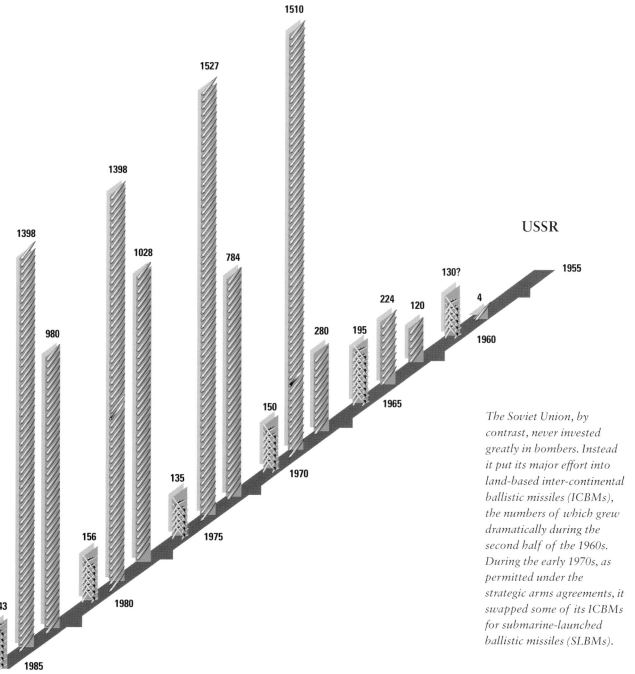

USSR

The Soviet Union, by contrast, never invested greatly in bombers. Instead it put its major effort into land-based inter-continental ballistic missiles (ICBMs), the numbers of which grew dramatically during the second half of the 1960s. During the early 1970s, as permitted under the strategic arms agreements, it swapped some of its ICBMs for submarine-launched ballistic missiles (SLBMs).

CHAPTER FOUR

VIETNAM

*THE BEAUTIFUL BUDDHIST TEMPLE of Angkor Wat in
Cambodia survived years of devastating war surprisingly
undamaged. Khmer Rouge soldiers guard the temple, which
they used as a hide-out, with a Russian heavy machine gun.*

VIETNAM

Two leading theorists of revolutionary guerrilla warfare meet when Ernesto 'Che' Guevara, at this time a minister in the Cuban government, visits Mao Tse-tung in China during an official visit in 1960. Mao's theories stood the test of time somewhat better than Che's.

GUERRILLA WARFARE

The consensus view in the United States in the early 1960s was that the Cold War had moved beyond the developed world into the developing. The upheavals of decolonization and the drive for economic modernization often aggravated social and political divisions and provided opportunities for radical groups. The United States took pride in its own revolutionary traditions and some made the optimistic assumption that this would impress Third World progressives. The revolutionary mantle, however, soon fell away when Washington had to decide whether to continue to support an established anti-communist ruling élite even when it showed scant interest in land reform and social justice. This tension was reflected in the *counter-insurgency* theories which so excited John Kennedy in 1961. According to these theories the key requirement for defeating an insurgency was to separate the fighters from the broad mass of the population who might otherwise sustain them and provide recruits. Programmes of economic and social reform could work on 'hearts and minds' but required enlightened élites. Faced with a regime unwilling to accept the logic of reform, the best that could be done was to eliminate as many as possible of the guerrillas, deterring new recruits through the prospect of capture or death. The trouble here was that guerrillas capable of merging with the local population would invite indiscriminate attacks, intensifying popular anger with the regime, so generating yet more support and recruits.

During the 1960s American counter-insurgency theory was put to the test against two different types of insurgent. The most romantic variety was epitomized by Che Guevara, an Argentinian who had been part of Castro's band in Cuba and went on to attempt, unsuccessfully, to foment revolution in Africa and in Bolivia. The Cuban approach was for the impatient. It was built

on the idea of the *foco* – a small group of dedicated men – able to stimulate an insurrection on its own by forcing the state to reveal its inner brutality while demonstrating the availability of an alternative, more sympathetic government. This theory arose out of a misreading of the Cuban revolution. Castro's success against the dictator Batista had been based both on the latter's unpopularity and on the moderation of Castro's own political programme, in contrast to the

Marxism–Leninism which he later proclaimed. Castro was able to survive as a substantial opposition leader with the help of his guerrilla band. It is by no means clear that with an explicitly Marxist programme he would have enjoyed such success. Certainly the experience of those who sought to apply the *foco* theory later on, as self-confessed Marxist–Leninists, failed miserably. This included Che Guevara himself, who died in Bolivia in 1967, executed on the direct orders of the Bolivian president, and thereafter a legend as a photogenic martyr.

Latin American regimes, supported by the United States, dealt with Cuban tactics successfully during the 1960s. In the end the Americans had far more trouble with an alternative approach to guerrilla warfare, largely developed by the Chinese leader Mao Tse-tung, during his campaigns against his nationalist opponents as well as the Japanese armies of occupation during the Second World War. Mao argued the need to develop patiently a firm political base, which required propaganda work and organization as well as a sensitivity to local conditions. To Mao it was unthinkable that a guerrilla group could even hope to survive without this sort of political work; it was sheer arrogance to believe that success could be achieved merely by arriving in a village, waving rifles and shouting slogans. As Mao explained the relationship of the guerrillas to the

Che's body is carried into a wash-house at Vallegrande Airfield in Bolivia to be cleaned up before being displayed to the world's media. He was shot by the Bolivian Army after his small and ineffectual band had been overwhelmed in a fight.

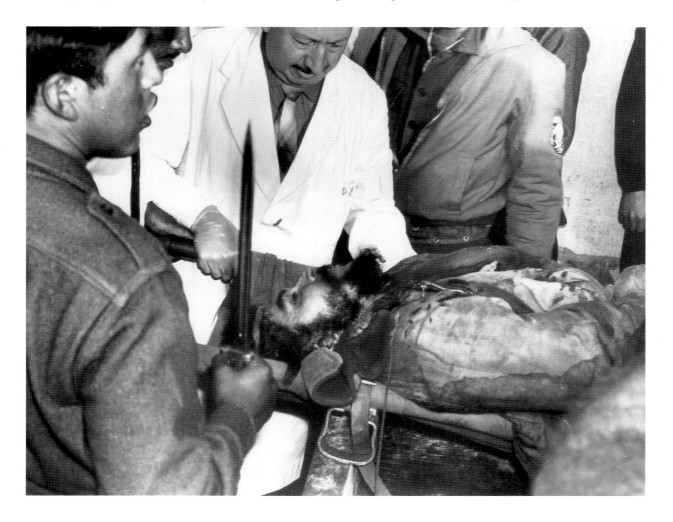

This 1969 calendar from the height of the Cultural Revolution conveys how it was promoted by elevating Mao to an icon, giving his sayings (carried around for easy reference in the 'little red book') a quasi-religious status and enthusing young people. The propaganda showed happy smiling faces, but the reality was of divided families, wrecked lives, neglect of education and economic decline.

people, it should be like that of the fish to the sea. Because this was the strategy of the militarily weak, unable to hold or seize territory through conventional battle, engagements with the enemy should be on favourable terms – ambushes rather than set-piece confrontations. Mao had explained his approach as early as 1930: 'Divide our forces to arouse the masses, concentrate our forces to deal with the enemy. The enemy advances, we retreat; the enemy camps, we harass; the enemy tires, we attack; the enemy retreats, we pursue.' Only when the enemy's will had been weakened would it be time to move to a stage of open warfare.

Maoist tactics succeeded against the American-backed nationalists in China. They were then applied by the Vietnamese, as adapted by General Vo Nguyen Giap. Like the Chinese, the North Vietnamese were prepared to play a long game. They began with the French, who returned after the Second World War to reclaim their Indo-Chinese colonies (Cambodia, Laos and Vietnam). The Communists

The world is yours, as well as ours, but in the last analysis, it is yours. You young people, full of vigour and vitality, are in the bloom of life, like the sun at eight or nine in the morning. Our hope is placed on you.

MAO TSE-TUNG

Chairman Mao and Vice-Chairman Lin among the Red Guards.

February   1 2 3 4 5 6 7 8 9 10 11 12 13 14 15 16 17 18 19 20 21 22 23 24 25 26 27 28

could take on the mantle of nationalists. This they did successfully, as the Vietminh, under the leadership of Ho Chi Minh. Initially the French succeeded in pushing them out of their northern strongholds and then moved on to dislodge them from their redoubt in the north-east. The Vietminh survived, and received a boost from Mao's victory in China. They then began to push directly against the French, but after being defeated in conventional engagements in 1951 they returned to guerrilla operations. The French garrison at Dien Bien Phu in late 1953 was put under siege by the communist forces and fell in May 1954. Although the Vietminh, led by Giap, had taken more casualties – 20,000 as against 7,000 – the political blow to the French, just as an international conference had convened at Geneva to settle the Korean and Indo-Chinese conflicts, was much greater. This brought home an important political lesson: success in such warfare was to be measured in political effects rather than military damage. Victory was as likely to go to those with the strongest motivation to succeed as to those with the greatest resources to apply.

PROPPING UP DIEM

The Geneva settlement divided Vietnam into two independent states at the 17th Parallel, with the Vietminh gaining control of the North, led by Ho Chi Minh, and a non-communist government installed in the South. In principle unification was to take place under democratic elections, but neither side demonstrated great interest in such a method. The South was led by Ngo Dinh Diem, who had a Catholic, mandarin, nationalist background and had been hailed as a modernizing leader. He was challenged by a Southern-based insurgency, proclaimed in 1960 as the National Liberation Front (soon to be known as the Vietcong). This was indigenous, although as the conflict dragged on, the autonomy of the Southern leaders declined. Diem believed that the North was the real source of all his problems. Under American guidance, he prepared to block a conventional invasion from the North. This focus, and the increasing sectarianism and repression exhibited by Diem's regime, helped the guerrillas to establish themselves in the South and to challenge governmental authority (often by murdering its local representatives).

The Kennedy administration accepted Eisenhower's commitment to prevent further advances by the communists in East Asia. This was the time of the 'domino theory' – the idea that if one state fell to communism, there would be a knock-on effect throughout the region, with one friendly government after another being toppled. So serious was the concern that for a while Kennedy was even prepared to send troops to the land-locked country of Laos in order to prevent its domination by the Pathet Lao, a communist group backed by the North Vietnamese. This was despite the weakness of the rightist forces in Laos and

Ngo Dinh Diem (1901–63) was a well-respected and independent politician who became prime minister of South Vietnam after the 1954 Geneva Accords and later president. He became increasingly autocratic and unpopular. Here he sits calmly, although this is a picture of him taken at a fair near Saigon just after a failed assassination attempt.

The two most renowned
North Vietnamese leaders,
President Ho Chi Minh
and General Vo Nguyen
Giap, look cheerful as
they inspect a unit of the
North Vietnamese Army
in training. Ho
(1890–1969), as the
founder of the Indo-
China Communist Party
was instrumental in
giving Asian communism
its nationalist orientation
and peasant basis. Giap
was the mastermind
behind the victory at Dien
Bien Phu in 1954 and
commanded North
Vietnamese forces against
the American-backed
South, employing both
guerrilla warfare and
conventional operations.

The essence of the campaigns, masterminded by the communists against first the French and then the South Vietnamese government and their American allies, was to control as much as possible of the countryside. When their enemies moved out from the cities the South Vietnamese and their allies could not cope with adept guerrillas and often resorted to crude methods, such as destroying areas where communists had been present, thereby adding to local people's opposition to the government. The Americans sought to weaken the guerrillas by interdicting the supply routes that supported them, of which the most notorious was the so-called Ho Chi Minh Trail, which moved through areas of Laos also under communist control, bypassing the notional border set in 1954 as a demilitarized zone, before moving into South Vietnam. The effort was never successful, because the trail was never a single road or river crossing that could be easily cut but a diffuse collection of paths, but also because guerrillas were often able to keep themselves well supplied locally and through weapons and ammunition captured from enemy forces.

the logistical problems of inserting American troops in any number. Eventually Kennedy was content to back a neutralist leader, acknowledged at least initially by Moscow if not by Hanoi. Inevitably, by not making a stand in Laos, Kennedy was compounding his problems in South Vietnam. The communists were able to use routes through Laos to infiltrate cadres into the South. More seriously, the impression might gain ground that when it came to the crunch he was not prepared to honour the unconditional promise of his inaugural address.

In Saigon Diem tried to play on Kennedy's desire not to appear weak. Yet Kennedy did not believe that the South Vietnamese government needed American combat troops to cope with the Vietcong and, despite a certain amount of lobbying from his advisers, never wavered in this view. He was, however, prepared to send increasing numbers of advisers. The build-up began in early 1962, and by the time of his assassination in November 1963 the numbers had grown from 685 to 16,732. In addition he believed that Diem should follow a 'hearts and minds' strategy, including serious political and economic reform. Diem showed no interest. Instead his regime became steadily more authoritarian. Local dissent

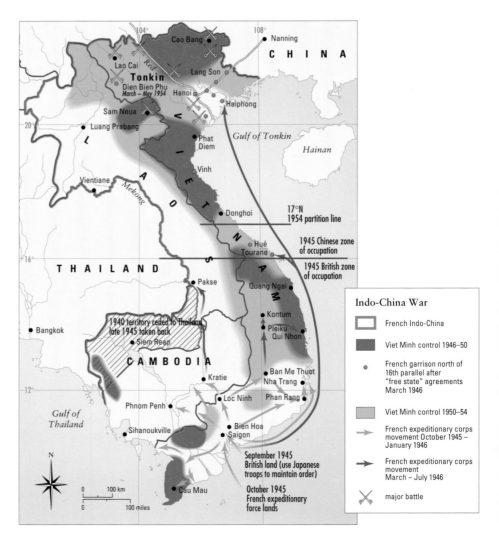

CHINA

BURMA

Cao Bang •
• Nanning
Lao Cai •
Lang Son
Tonkin
Dien Bien Phu •
Hanoi •
Haiphong •
Sam Neua •
Gulf of Tonkin
Luang Prabang •
Hainan
Mekong
• Phat Diem
• Vinh
Vientiane •
Yankee Station
US 7th fleet
• Donghoi
Mekong
DMZ
• Hue
THAILAND
• Tourane
• Pakse
I CORPS
Quang Ngai •
• Kontum
• Pleiku
• Qui Nhon
II CORPS
• Bangkok
• Siem Reap
• Ban Me Thuot
• Nha Trang
CAMBODIA
• Kratie
Dixie Station
• Phnom Penh
• Loc Ninh
III CORPS
• Phan Rang
• Sihanoukville
• Bien Hoa
■ Saigon
IV CORPS
1975 US military evacuation
• Cau Mau

Gulf of Thailand

N

0   100 km
0   100 miles

Vietnam War
1959–75

Communist-held area January 1973 'ceasefire'

– ‑ – US corps command area

✳ North Vietnam subject to air attack

Communist-controlled area in Laos and Cambodia 1950–75

controlled by Khmer Rouge c. 1975

controlled by Pathet Lao c. 1975

area of Communist guerrilla activity c. 1975

Communist supply routes

→ Ho Chi Minh Trail

→ Sihanouk Trail

–‑► sea supply routes

▨ Communist-held area 1959–60

NORTH VIETNAM

CHINA

• Ha Giang
• Nanning
• Hanoi
• Haiphong
Gulf of Tonkin
• Nam Dinh
• Ninh Binh
Hainan
• Thanh Hoa
• Yulin
• Vinh
Nape Pass
• HaTinh
Mu Gia Pass
Ben Kari Pass
• Dong Hoi
• Thakhek
DMZ
• Quang Tri
• Tchepone
• Khe Sanh
• Savannakhet
• Hué
LAOS
• Da Nang
• Quang Ngai
• Ubon Ratchathani
• Kontum
• Qui Nhon
CAMBODIA (KAMPUCHEA)
• Battambang
• Pursat
• Kratie
• Nha Trang
• Kompong Chhnang
• Cam Ranh Bay
• Kompong Cham
SOUTH VIETNAM
Gulf of Thailand
• Phnom Penh
• Ho Chi Minh (Saigon)
Kompong Som (Sihanoukville)
• My Tho
• Can Tho
• Vonh Loi

2000
1000
500
200
0 m

South China Sea

grew and more coups were plotted. For much of 1962 and 1963 this failure was obscured from the Americans by the adoption of what seemed like a sensible counter-insurgency policy based on strategic hamlets, safe areas to which the rural population could go to escape communists and eke out their living. The hamlets, however, were built in a rush to help Diem and his family consolidate their political control, and they provided no real bulwark against Vietcong advances once the guerrillas had worked out how to undermine them.

For most of his presidency Kennedy paid scant attention to Vietnam. He did not want to move against Diem, whom he had backed in the past as a strong leader. There was no reason to suppose that any alternative would be much better. On the other hand, Diem's methods, and especially those of his brother, were causing widespread dismay in the United States. From the summer of 1963 the regime began to be drained of support. Diem had made powerful enemies among the American press corps. They questioned the official line that the campaign against the communists was going extremely well, and openly despised the American mission in Saigon (capital of South Vietnam, now Ho Chi Minh City) for parroting these claims despite so much evidence to the contrary. The regime's harassment of the media added to their contempt. That summer, capitalizing on this antagonism, Buddhists in Saigon began to protest openly,

At a press conference in March 1961 President Kennedy tries to explain the threat posed by communists to the cohesion of Laos. He warned that if the communist Pathet Lao did not stop their attacks 'those who support a truly neutral Laos will have to consider their response'.

using the dramatic method of self-immolation to highlight their cause. The response was more repression. By October the Americans were putting serious pressure on Diem to get him to change his ways. The Americans were aware of new plots among generals to dispose of Diem. They did not stop these and, while they did not give them active support either, the open evidence of American irritation with the South Vietnamese leader steadily undermined his standing. He remained stubborn, but then became the victim of another coup led by generals now convinced that the Americans would do nothing to spare their former client. On 1 November 1963 he was assassinated along with his brother.

AFTER THE ASSASSINATIONS

The assassination of President Kennedy took place on 22 November 1963, just three weeks after that of Diem. The American political leadership changed before a new Vietnamese leadership had time to settle. The new president, Lyndon Baines Johnson, had been opposed to any association at all with the plotters against Diem, and saw Kennedy's assassination almost as retribution for this folly. The position certainly did not improve under a new military regime. Soon there was yet another coup within the military junta, leaving General Nguyen Khanh as premier. There was a sense that the Americans had little choice but to make this their war. This was combined with evidence that the situation in the country was deteriorating. Only just after Kennedy died was the veil lifted and the optimism that had characterized the military reporting from Vietnam shown to be unreliable and misleading. Morale was poor and the Vietcong were making inroads.

It may have been hard for the Americans to walk away from South Vietnam but no more so than attempting to generate an aura of legitimacy around a chronically unstable and inept regime. Reforming the South and producing an effective campaign against the communists was going to take time, and any achievements would have to be earned in the face of incessant subversion. On the doubtful assumption that all communist activity in the South was directed from the North, senior Americans began to argue that the best way to stop the rot in the South would be to target the North.

What might this achieve? If North Vietnam really controlled the Vietcong then there might be ways to interfere with logistical support for the guerrillas, or else air power might be employed to inflict pain on the North so as to coerce it to abandon the Vietcong, or at least make some concessions in peace negotiations. There were a number of difficulties with each of these aspirations. The Vietcong were able to sustain their campaign without supplies from the North. They captured the bulk of their weapons from the South Vietnamese Army. If, as a result of American air raids, the North decided to intensify rather than run down its efforts on the ground, then the South Vietnamese would be unable to cope. There were more serious dangers: if the Americans took the war to the North there was a risk that the Chinese could be forced to join in on Hanoi's behalf, just

A photograph that changed history. Malcolm Browne of Associated Press took this photograph as a 73-year-old Buddhist monk sought to protest against the persecution of Buddhists in South Vietnam by dousing himself in petrol and setting fire to himself. The Americans put pressure on Diem to respond to the Buddhists' demands and bring in political reform. His refusal to do so widened the rift with Washington.

as they had joined North Korea. To reduce this risk the Americans would have to pull their punches, thereby draining the air campaign of much of its impact. Yet even if Hanoi wished to avoid the pain and accepted the need for negotiations, Saigon's hand would still be extremely weak because of its limited control over its own territory. As it happens Hanoi had been deliberating about the possibility of doing some deal with the South so as to cut out the Americans, offering non-communists a modest role in a new government. There had been some discussion with the French and Poles, and possibly even Diem's brother, in 1963, but Diem had never been strong enough on his own to see this through. This was even more true of his successors. So while the Americans looked to put pressure on the North to help bring stability to the South, exerting such pressure would carry high risks without a more stable South.

When eventually a bombing campaign began against the North the pessimists were vindicated almost immediately. Why then did the air campaign begin in early 1965? Part of the answer may be hubris. American power was at a peak. The successful resolution of the Cuban missile crisis had given American policy-makers new confidence in their capacity to manage any crisis. The United States appeared to have surged ahead in the nuclear-arms race and, while the country had been stunned by the murder of its president, Johnson had moved skilfully to enact civil rights legislation and was promising, in his Great Society programme, an era of domestic harmony and shared prosperity. At the same time, the Soviet model was already showing signs of the bureaucratic paralysis that would lead to its eventual demise. It was hard to believe that a poor, communist country that had already endured years of war and hardship would not buckle when confronted with the full might of the United States.

Part of this confidence was reflected in the more elaborate strategic theories developed to cope with the paradoxes of the nuclear age, which stressed the coercive potential of threats to hurt and the ability to manipulate military power, using it to send complex political signals rather than simply indulge in displays of brute force. This confidence was reinforced by the Gulf of Tonkin incident in August 1964 when it was alleged that North Vietnamese patrol boats in the Gulf had twice attacked the destroyer USS *Maddox*. The first attack was in response to covert (and CIA-directed) South Vietnamese operations against the North's coast nearby, which had in part been intended to be a provocative show of force and about which the destroyer's commander was unaware, and the second attack is now believed not to have occurred. In reprisal President Johnson ordered air raids against torpedo-boat bases and supporting facilities in the North. This was believed to be precisely the sort of action which would have political eloquence, warning Hanoi to back off yet without becoming a major operation. It had a domestic political advantage as well. Johnson used it to get *carte blanche* from Congress, in the form of a resolution which allowed him 'to take all necessary measures to repel any armed attack against the forces of the United States and to prevent further aggression'.

For the next few months little happened. Johnson was campaigning in the November 1964 presidential election as a man of peace. He easily defeated the hawkish Republican candidate, Barry Goldwater. While the election was under way options were being clarified for later action in Vietnam. The three options identified were to continue with present policies, leading, it was widely assumed, to eventual withdrawal; to follow the military preference for a systematic programme of military pressures against the North, presumably with a political purpose as the achievable military purposes were unclear; and to undertake a combination of diplomatic communications and graduated military moves designed to force Hanoi into negotiations. One way or another the Americans wanted to impress Hanoi with their commitment, yet they were not truly resolute. The problem remained one of shoring up a rotten regime against a determined opponent. Whether or not the South Vietnamese government deserved extra American military support, it was not clear that it could cope with it. South Vietnam was sliding steadily downhill.

In January 1965 the president was persuaded that it was pointless waiting for the South to stabilize before taking the war to the North. Perhaps, it was

In April 1968, weary from leading his country through an unpopular war and recognizing that he might not be re-elected in that year's presidential election, Lyndon Johnson announced that he would not seek his party's nomination and that he was ending the bombing with a view to starting peace talks with North Vietnam.

suggested, what Saigon needed was evidence that the power of the United States was being unleashed on its behalf. This might convince the anti-communist forces in the South to pull together and work for victory. The air campaign against the North was designed not with Hanoi so much as Saigon in mind. In February 1965 an attack on the US base at Pleiku, killing eight Americans and wounding sixty more, provided sufficient pretext and led to an immediate, co-ordinated air strike against four army bases in southern North Vietnam. Soon there was a communist reprisal against an American base, and then the Americans moved into a limited air campaign. Targets could be chosen to avoid the risk of Chinese intervention, but not to prevent the North seeking to destabilize further the South. The American intelligence agencies warned that this would be the likely communist response, and that it was unclear whether the South could cope.

In the middle of the deliberations on the policy there was yet more political unrest in Vietnam, delaying the start of the air strikes. The first raids of what became known as Operation Rolling Thunder began on 2 March. Sorties eventually grew from a hundred per month in March 1965 to as many as 12,000 per month by September 1966. The campaign failed to compel the North Vietnamese to cease supporting the insurgency in the South, nor did it interfere with the flow of men and *matériel* to the insurgents. As had been feared, the air campaign spurred the North to even greater efforts to achieve a quick victory, or at least claim ground in case there was a serious peace negotiation. Although the Americans had seen an air campaign as, in some sense, an alternative to employing ground forces in a combat role, the surge of communist activity led inexorably to American involvement in the land war, initially just to protect their own bases. In the summer of 1965 US troops were formally committed to combat. Total US troop strength reached 215,000 by February 1966 (it eventually reached 525,000). Australia and South Korea also agreed to send troops.

ROLLING THUNDER TO LINEBACKER

The Vietcong's guerrilla operations continued mainly in the Central Highlands and the Mekong Delta district. In principle the best way to deal with these should have been through a 'hearts and minds' campaign designed to separate the Vietcong from the broad mass of the population, the fish from the sea. There were limitations to this approach so long as the government in Saigon lacked a popular base. At any rate the United States Army preferred traditional military methods and adopted a 'search and destroy' strategy designed to impose maximum attrition on the Vietcong. The constant risk with this strategy was that the imperfect means available for distinguishing between communists and non-communists, and targeting the communists once they had been identified, led to the civilian population feeling the brunt of the war and progressively losing sympathy with the government.

The size of the American operation was sufficient to prevent defeat but not enough to deliver victory. The best the Americans could hope for was that the communists would attempt to win a conventional battle. Ironically, when this happened the American and South Vietnamese forces did indeed win, but the result was a political defeat. By the start of 1968, after over two years of fighting the superior resources and firepower of the West, the communists felt that their position was starting to become precarious. On 30 January 1968, as a desperate gamble, they launched the Tet Offensive. The insurgents took the war right into the heart of the leading cities of the South. They achieved none of their immediate objectives and suffered massive casualties, but they did succeed in hitting American public opinion, reached via television cameras. Already frustrated at the cost and length of the war, and having been fed optimistic reports of the situation on the ground, it was suddenly treated to pictures of ferocious fighting in many Vietnamese cities, including Saigon and the old imperial capital of Hue, where fighting was especially fierce. The war was now tearing American society apart as youngsters sought to avoid the draft and engaged in increasingly radical protests, challenging not only the war, but the Cold War

The comparative size of the captured American airman and his small Vietnamese guard, as shown on page 6, was used by North Vietnam to show how it would achieve victory against a much stronger opponent.

assumptions behind it and the political system that had allowed these assumptions to take hold. In April 1968 a shaken Lyndon Johnson opted out of the coming presidential election and proposed ceasefire talks. The invitation was accepted by the North and the talks were convened in Paris in May 1968. In October a bombing halt was ordered to help improve the atmosphere.

The Nixon administration intended to end America's war in Vietnam and expected to do so without this taking up the whole of the president's first term. At the very least the president sought to reduce the level of US participation in the hope that casualties would drop. This was to be achieved through Vietnamization – that is, strengthening the ability of the South Vietnamese Army's front-line combat forces to cope without American support. It was announced on 20 April 1969 when Nixon stated that he would withdraw 150,000 men from Vietnam during the next year. Three years later, by April 1972, US force levels had fallen from 543,000 at the start of the administration to 69,000. The US death rate had fallen by a tenth from its 1968 peak of 300 per week, although there were still 50,000 casualties during the Nixon years. In addition, conscription was to end in 1973, thereby removing another of the causes that had fuelled discontent.

The strain of war is clearly etched on the face of an old woman and the soldier helping her escape.

Vietcong Commando attack on the US Embassy
30 January 1968

US Consulate buildings

helip

front gate

4

1

Vietcong vehicles

1 Vietcong commandos besiege US embassy, driving US guards into building

2 US 101st airborne helicopters attempted relief is driven off

3 Vietcong breach the wall, infiltrating embassy grounds

4 US reinforcements finally break siege and kill remaining Vietcong around embassy

THE TET OFFENSIVE

This was a remarkable example of a political victory emerging out of a military defeat. After senior American commanders had claimed, correctly, that their forces were steadily wearing the communists down, it came as something of a shock when the Vietcong suddenly appeared in the South's major cities. Even the American embassy compound in Saigon itself was under siege for a while. The attacks were suicidal, and the Vietcong never really recovered from the offensive, but American confidence was badly shaken and soon President Johnson resigned and peace talks were set in motion.

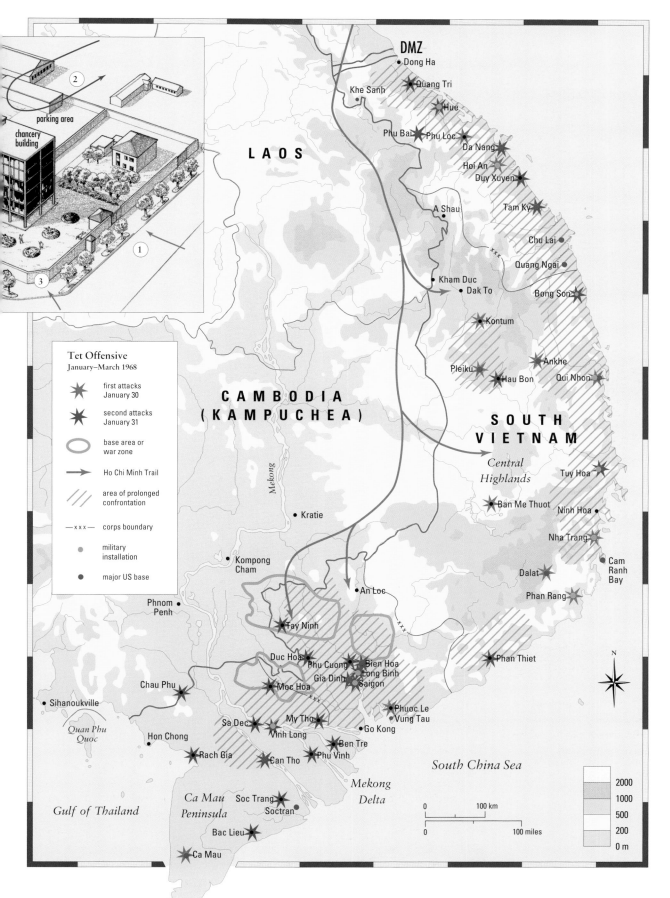

parking area

chancery
building

2

1

3

DMZ

• Dong Ha

✦ Quang Tri

• Khe Sanh

✦ Hue

Phu Bai ✦ Phu Loc

✦ Da Nang

Hoi An ✦

Duy Xuyen ✦

• A Shau

Tam Ky ✦

LAOS

Chu Lai •

Quang Ngai •

• Kham Duc

xxx

• Dak To

Bong Son ✦

✦ Kontum

**SOUTH
VIETNAM**

Ankhe ✦

Pleiku •

✦ Hau Bon

Qui Nhon •

Tet Offensive
January–March 1968

✦ first attacks
January 30

✦ second attacks
January 31

◯ base area or
war zone

→ Ho Chi Minh Trail

/// area of prolonged
confrontation

—xxx— corps boundary

• military
installation

● major US base

**CAMBODIA
(KAMPUCHEA)**

*Central
Highlands*

Tuy Hoa ✦

✦ Ban Me Thuot

Ninh Hoa •

Nha Trang ✦

Dalat ✦

Cam
Ranh
Bay

Phan Rang ✦

• Kratie

Mekong

• Kompong
Cham

• An Loc

Phnom
Penh •

✦ Tay Ninh

xxx

Phan Thiet ✦

N

Chau Phu ✦

Duc Hoa ✦

Phu Cuong •

Gia Dinh •

Bien Hoa ✦
Long Binh ●
Saigon ●

Moc Hoa ✦

xxx

Phuoc Le ✦
Vung Tau •

• Sihanoukville

Sa Dec ✦

My Tho ✦

• Go Kong

*Quan Phu
Quoc*

Hon Chong •

Vinh Long ✦

Ben Tre ✦

Rach Gia ✦

Can Tho ✦ Phu Vinh ✦

South China Sea

0   100 km

*Ca Mau
Peninsula*

Soc Trang ✦

Soctran •

*Mekong
Delta*

0   100 miles

Gulf of Thailand

Bac Lieu ✦

2000
1000
500
200
0 m

✦ Ca Mau

Nixon hoped to use the Paris negotiations to give Saigon a fighting chance following a total American withdrawal. The message to North Vietnam was that it should be satisfied if it got the United States out of Vietnam; it could not expect Washington to hand over Saigon on a plate. Accordingly, he demanded that all communist forces withdraw from the South. The only way this log jam was ever going to be broken was when each side accepted that it could not eliminate the other. Thus although a negotiating framework existed in Paris, the incentives for a negotiated outcome did not. This became apparent even when a secret channel was opened in August 1969 between Dr Henry Kissinger, Nixon's national security adviser, and senior North Vietnamese figures, most notably Le Duc Tho. This secret connection was halted abruptly by Hanoi in October 1971, having achieved no more than the Paris talks.

Yet the American negotiating position was weakening because of US troop withdrawals. Nixon could not weaken Hanoi militarily but he hoped to do so politically through isolation. During the course of the Vietnam War the

communist world had suffered traumatic upheavals as a result of the end of the Sino-Soviet alliance. During the mid 1960s Chairman Mao not only took China into the nuclear age, with an atomic bomb being tested in 1964 and a thermonuclear weapon barely three years later, but at the same time launched the 'Cultural Revolution', which was designed to prevent the country becoming stifled by bureaucracy and materialism. The United States and the Soviet Union were denounced as two sides of the same coin. Suddenly the long Soviet border with China became a flashpoint, and the two sides built up massive armed forces. In 1969 there were even skirmishes along the Amur and Ussuri rivers. There was a fear that these could escalate into something much worse until, at Ho Chi Minh's funeral in Hanoi that September, Chinese and Russian leaders agreed to calm things down. Although the Vietnam débâcle had weakened the United States, the sudden emergence of this new threat to the East challenged the Soviet Union, and so it was not that surprising to find these two superpowers working on a form of détente at this time, especially as both Europe and the arms race appeared to have

American troops run to board a helicopter in May 1966. Although the United States had made substantial use of helicopters in Korea, it was in Vietnam that they showed their worth, with the Huey (Bell UH-1 Iroquois) serving as a means of moving infantry units quickly, keeping them supplied, evacuating casualties and supporting ground attacks.

acquired a reinforcing stability. More surprising was the revelation in 1971 that Kissinger had visited Beijing.

The 'Cultural Revolution' had turned Chinese society upside down, encouraging educational and technical backwardness. After a power struggle which led to the defeat of the militants, the old guard began to get a grip on the situation. The surprising overture from Washington had come as they were wondering what to do about China's political isolation. The breakthrough in 1971 was followed by a visit by Nixon to Beijing, extraordinary in the light of Nixon's rise to power as a stern anti-communist. The Chinese and Americans were working not so much on ideology as on old *realpolitik* principles: my enemy's enemy is my friend. The Americans now had the opportunity to play the two communist states off against each other and their intended victim in this was North Vietnam. Hanoi undoubtedly was dismayed by the turn of events.

The North's new vulnerability became apparent in April 1972. The communists had just recovered sufficiently from the 1968 Tet Offensive to launch another major ground attack. Hanoi hoped to seize territory and demonstrate the futility of Vietnamization, and so lead Nixon to abandon the South Vietnamese leader, General Nguyen Van Thieu, who had taken charge in the summer of 1965. On 30 March 1972, North Vietnamese divisions moved on to the offensive. This was no longer guerrilla warfare but a conventional attack supported by both tanks and long-range artillery. Almost the whole of the North Vietnamese Army was involved. The North achieved the element of surprise by successfully hiding the transportation of tanks through Cambodia, and also because attacks of this type and magnitude were unprecedented. But its commanders lacked the strategic concepts for this sort of fighting and the weight of numbers to press home their advantage. Despite some initial successes the offensive soon faltered. The South Vietnamese Army was now a much more serious fighting prospect than it had been earlier in the war. It threw everything into the fight.

A critical difference lay in the American air campaign. For the first time B-52s were used to attack targets near Hanoi and Haiphong, including Haiphong's oil storage facilities and Haiphong harbour (where four Soviet ships were hit). Kissinger was told to emphasize his tough stance to both Hanoi and Moscow. Nixon was relying on the Soviet desire for détente – a major summit was planned for that May in Moscow, when all manner of arms control agreements were planned. Although Hanoi remained intransigent, when Nixon launched the next stage of the air campaign,

Nixon in Beijing. The president stands beside Prime Minister Chou Enlai during the course of his historic visit to China in February 1972. Chou (1898–1976), a long-time comrade of Mao, was one of the few moderating factors during the Cultural Revolution and played an active role in bringing its excesses to an end.

known as Operation Linebacker 1, on 8 May, the Soviet premier, Leonid Brezhnev, did not withdraw his invitation to Moscow. From 9 May to 23 October the United States made 41,500 attack sorties on North Vietnam. This was the first large-scale use of what came to be known as 'smart' bombs – that is those with a high degree of precision guidance – and these did upset the resupply effort in ways that had hitherto not been possible. Hanoi found its ground offensive in trouble because supplies were hampered, while because of the mining of Haiphong harbour it faced problems in importing food and vital resources into the North. So unlike Rolling Thunder, Linebacker 1 made a difference. In critical areas it supported the South Vietnamese Army by making it possible for it to resist and rebuff the North's advance. Politically it confirmed that Moscow (and for that matter Beijing) now put its relations with the United States as a top priority.

The failure of the offensive left the North weakened and it agreed to revive the negotiations. Before it launched another offensive it would need to build up its strength once again and, if possible, get rid of American air power. Kissinger was anxious to do a quick deal. Whereas Nixon's position might be stronger after the November 1972 elections (and he won easily), Congress had also banned appropriations after 31 December 1972 'for the purpose of engaging U.S. forces, land, sea or air, in hostilities in Indochina'. His problem was in persuading Thieu to accept what he could negotiate. The North was no longer demanding Thieu's resignation or the cessation of all American aid to his regime. But Kissinger's secrecy had left Thieu unprepared for a negotiated breakthrough and

Nixon in Moscow. With his hand strengthened by his visit to China, Nixon felt able to play one communist giant off against the other. In May 1972 an interpreter helps President Nixon exchange pleasantries with President Nikolai Podgorny and General Secretary Leonid Brezhnev.

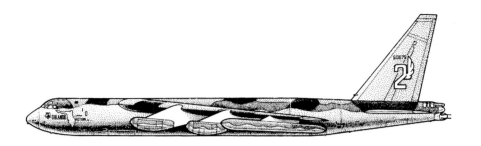

THE B-52 BOMBER

Although designed for nuclear use, the B-52's massive load-carrying capacity of 488,000 pounds enabled it to drop conventional bombs of up to 2,000 pounds on to Vietnam. With a range of 8,800 miles, and a top speed of 650 mph, it could operate from bases well away from Vietnam.

uncommitted to a deal that left communist forces below the 17th Parallel or his security in any way dependent upon the communists keeping their word. On 26 October 1972 Kissinger gave a press conference, declaring that 'peace is at hand'. The tone, just before an election, was misleading, as Thieu was refusing to go along with the deal and Hanoi was not making any more concessions. To get Thieu on board he was offered massive amounts of military equipment but at the same time warned that he would be publicly blamed for a failure in the peace process. The administration was now bargaining with Thieu, and to win him round needed some concessions from Hanoi – which believed that it already had a deal with Kissinger. Nixon was determined that if necessary he would resume bombing the North to extract them.

Linebacker 2 was geared to inflict civilian distress without excessive casualties. B-52s would attack railyards, storage areas, power plants, communication centres and airfields located on Hanoi's periphery. Meanwhile air force and navy fighters attacked objectives in populated areas with smart bombs. The policy was a gamble. It depended on coercing the North and, feeling aggrieved, Hanoi might not negotiate. This was its initial response after the bombing began. There was also a major international outcry. Equally seriously, the US Air Force was taking risks with the campaign. Because there had been no time for defence suppression early losses of B-52s were high, while bad weather delayed some of the tactical air strikes. The bombing was described as 'war by

B-52 bombers attack Hanoi during the Linebacker 2 raids of December 1972. American aircraft faced 1,000 SAMs, as well as Mig fighters and anti-aircraft guns. During the raids 26 aircraft were lost, of which 15 were B-52s. Three were damaged. Of the 92 aircrew involved 26 were rescued, 33 were taken prisoner, 4 died in a crash landing and 29 were unaccounted for.

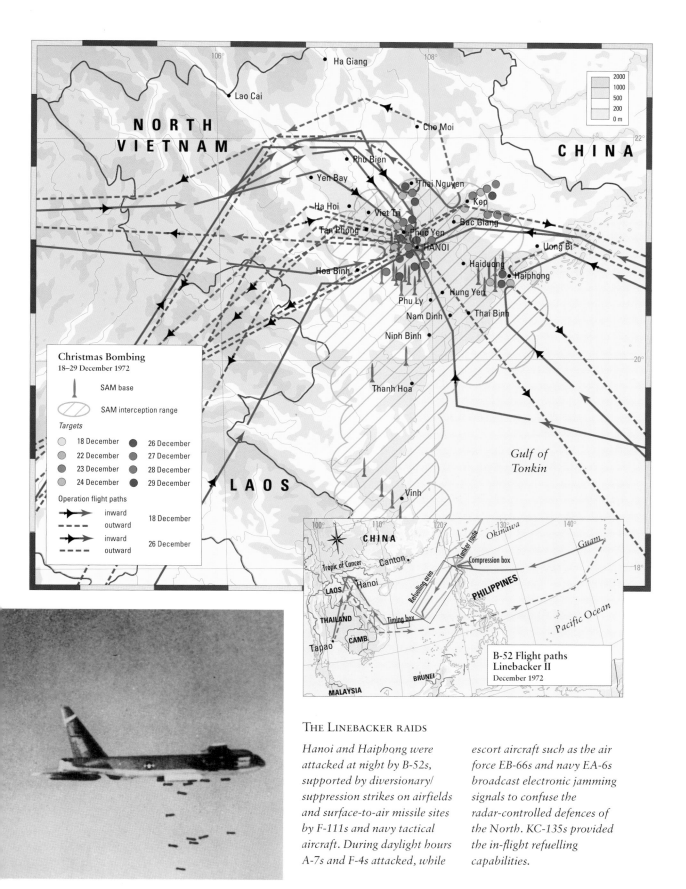

Christmas Bombing
18–29 December 1972

⊥	SAM base
⬭	SAM interception range

Targets

● 18 December	● 26 December
● 22 December	● 27 December
● 23 December	● 28 December
● 24 December	● 29 December

Operation flight paths

➤	inward	
--➤	outward	18 December
➤	inward	
--➤	outward	26 December

B-52 Flight paths
Linebacker II
December 1972

THE LINEBACKER RAIDS

Hanoi and Haiphong were attacked at night by B-52s, supported by diversionary/ suppression strikes on airfields and surface-to-air missile sites by F-111s and navy tactical aircraft. During daylight hours A-7s and F-4s attacked, while escort aircraft such as the air force EB-66s and navy EA-6s broadcast electronic jamming signals to confuse the radar-controlled defences of the North. KC-135s provided the in-flight refuelling capabilities.

The American defeat in Vietnam came to be symbolized by images from the end of April 1975 as the North Vietnamese took over Saigon and desperate South Vietnamese tried to get on board an American helicopter that could take them from the American embassy to navy ships off the coast.

tantrum', wanton, savage and senseless, a crime against humanity, and so on. The contrast with the pre-election claims could not have been starker. Nixon was worried that all could go badly wrong, and if Hanoi had agreed to resume negotiations, the North might have seen the bombing cut back. After a break for Christmas Day itself, on 26 December the bombing resumed with a vengeance. The B-52s were now used more carefully. One-hundred-and-twenty aircraft struck ten different targets in fifteen minutes. Hanoi was attacked from four directions and Haiphong from two. Massive raids over the next couple of days left the North crippled and exhausted. The North offered the required concessions. From 18 to 29 December B-52s flew 729 sorties against thirty-four targets north of the 20th Parallel and dropped 15,237 tons of bombs. Combining for 1,216 sorties, US Air Force and Navy fighters delivered roughly 5,000 tons of ordnance. In eleven days Linebacker 2 dropped 13 per cent of the total tonnage dropped in the five months of Linebacker 1. Between 1968 and 1972 there had been only 51,000 tactical and 9,800 B-52 sorties.

The Americans hoped that by demonstrating to Thieu how the USA could turn air power on and off he would be reassured and compliant. In fact it needed Nixon to threaten to sign the peace treaty, if necessary alone, to obtain Thieu's grudging signature. On 23 January 1973 the final deal was reached, in all essentials the same as the one agreed in October. The North agreed to release US

POWs and not increase its troops in the South. It also accepted the proposal for a mixed armistice commission to supervise the ceasefire. And the legitimacy of the South Vietnam government was accepted – so long as the legitimacy of the communist's Liberation Front was also acknowledged. Critically, the right of Northern troops to be in the South was agreed, and therefore their ability to influence the future course of the South's history. They would retain control of about 40 per cent of South's territory. The final B-52 sorties over Vietnam occurred on 27 January, the day of the peace settlement.

The agreement collapsed two years later with Nixon gone and the American public in no mood to act to save a South Vietnam incapable of looking after itself. A communist offensive in late 1974 led to a decision by the South Vietnamese government in March 1975 to abandon the northern provinces. This resulted in a severe drop in morale of its armed forces, which on paper ought still to have been a match for those of the communists. The whole country was soon under communist control, Saigon falling on 30 April. The communists had paid a high price: over 900,000 dead as opposed to fewer than 200,000 of the South Vietnamese. Some 46,000 Americans had been killed, 300,000 wounded and some $112 billion spent trying to save South Vietnam.

While the fall of the South did not have a domino effect throughout Asia – the best case now to be made for the American effort in Vietnam is that it bought

Prince Norodom Sihanouk, the Cambodian head of state, distanced himself from the United States during the Vietnam War. In 1970 he was overthrown and the pro-American Lon Nol took charge. Sihanouk created a government-in-exile in Beijing, allied with the North Vietnamese and the Khmer Rouge. He returned as head of state in 1975, when Lon Nol fled, but resigned a year later and was put under house arrest by Pol Pot (who killed his children and grandchildren). This picture shows a 1974 ceremony when China promised arms and supplies to Sihanouk's government. He stands in the middle beside Chou Enlai.

time for the rest of the region to be stabilized – it did see communist dominance of Indo-China. Laos and Cambodia soon fell to communist rule. Cambodia became the greatest victim of the communist triumph. It had been neutral since the Geneva Conference of 1954, but its head of state, Prince Norodom Sihanouk, had inclined towards the communists and allowed substantial numbers of North Vietnamese into his country. This drew the Americans into the war in a secret bombing campaign against the communist bases. With the internal political balance in Cambodia upset, Sihanouk was overthrown in an anti-communist coup led by General Lon Nol, who was soon fighting the communist Khmer

Rouge. When he needed help from the Americans it was not forthcoming: Congress was too annoyed about past deception. Lon Nol's resistance collapsed, with that of all non-communists, in April 1975.

The Khmer Rouge regime under Pol Pot soon became notorious for viciousness, with a campaign of genocide carried out against all those who did not fit his rigid ideological mode. Not even Hanoi could control his excesses, as his victory had not depended on its help and he was hostile to the idea of a Vietnamese hegemony. By 1978 border skirmishes had begun with Vietnam, whose patience was soon exhausted. At the end of the year it launched a massive attack using twelve divisions and had soon cut through all of Cambodia (now known as Kampuchea). By 7 January 1979 it was in control of Phnom Penh and soon held the major cities. Pol Pot's base was, however, rural. Some 60,000 Khmer Rouge fighters melted away into the countryside to conduct guerrilla operations.

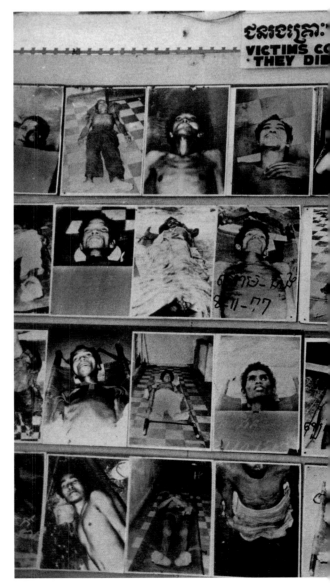

Pol Pot (1925–98) was a communist activist in Cambodia who had led the party since 1963, latterly as leader of the guerrilla force, the Khmer Rouge. He became prime minister in 1975 until pushed out by the Vietnamese Army in January 1979. He then continued to lead opposition to the Hanoi-imposed government in Phnom Penh as a guerrilla leader.

The internecine warfare in Asia continued as the Chinese, who were also anxious to prevent the establishment of a Greater Vietnam, decided that they would teach Hanoi a lesson. In March 1979 thirty-three Chinese divisions invaded, captured the provincial capital of Lang Son and then, almost as suddenly, withdrew to their own boundaries. Beijing said this was because the limited aims had been met. The Chinese also appear to have found Vietnamese forces, well equipped and fighting on excellent defensive terrain, something of a handful. This brought home to China the obsolescence of its equipment, logistical support and tactics (which often relied upon human waves). There were no further border incidents. The Vietnamese were left tied down on the Chinese border and inside Kampuchea. Instead of a series of civil wars across the Cold War divide in East Asia, the area had become the cockpit for a series of intra-communist civil wars.

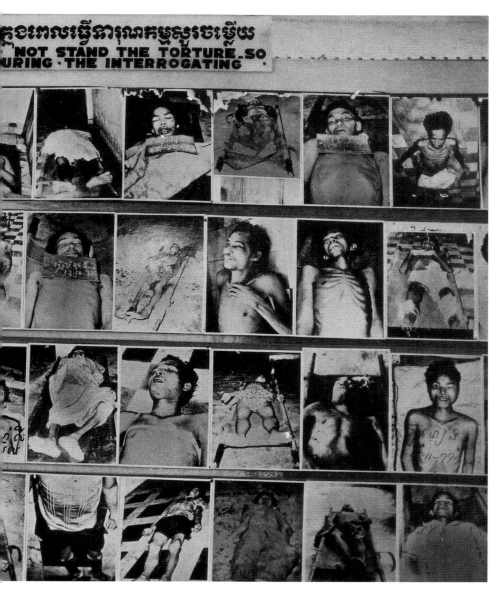

During the Khmer Rouge's reign of terror an estimated one million people died in Cambodia, many through executions. These photographs were taken by the Khmer Rouge at an 'extermination camp' near the capital Phnom Penh, where over 12,000 people died.

CHAPTER FIVE

DÉTENTE

TANKS OF INVADING RUSSIAN TROOPS in Wenceslas Square, Prague, in August 1968. The invasion undermined any suggestion that East and West could converge as Warsaw Pact countries reformed their economic and political practices, but it made no impact on the drive to reduce tensions between the two ideological blocs.

DÉTENTE

In November 1956 furious Hungarians burn pictures of Stalin in Budapest as Soviet forces march in to crush their rebellion. The revolution had begun on 23 October 1956 when police fired into a student demonstration, which led to a full-scale insurrection, with the army joining in.

SOVIET POWER

As the self-esteem of the United States buckled under the impact of Vietnam, Soviet power was reaching its zenith. The dogged Leonid Brezhnev, who had taken over from the turbulent Nikita Khrushchev in a Politburo coup in October 1964, had demonstrated a commitment to military strength and shown that he was prepared to use it. In 1968, in what became known as the 'Prague Spring', the old guard of the Czech Communist Party had suddenly been replaced by reformers, anxious to revive the economy by introducing liberalization both in the economy and in political life more generally. The new government, led by

Alexander Dubcek, was well aware of Russian sensitivity to any suggestion that the momentum of reform could take it out of the Warsaw Pact. In 1956 a similar, but much more tumultuous, movement in Hungary had been crushed by Soviet tanks and its leader, Imre Nagy, executed when the country appeared to be on the verge of moving out of the Soviet bloc. Yet despite the care taken not to challenge Moscow on this point, every liberal action represented an ideological affront, challenging the vanguard role of the Communist Party. In August 1968 the tanks moved in and orthodox communists were reinstated.

In 1956 NATO had appeared to urge the Nagy government on while being quite unable to help the Hungarians when the crackdown began. In 1968, therefore, the West was much more cautious. In fact relations with Moscow improved. In part this was also a consequence of the backwash from Vietnam,

On 1 November 1956 a new government led by a nationalist communist, Imre Nagy, announced Hungary's withdrawal from the Warsaw Pact. Soviet tanks, which had been leaving, returned and fighting broke out as Soviet troops slowly reimposed communist rule. Nagy was executed in 1958. Some 200,000 refugees escaped to the West.

which had left public opinion in Europe much less sure that it was really backing the right superpower and less inclined to invest in defence. Moreover, after the dramas over Berlin with which the 1960s began, there was a yearning for a quieter life. In a report for NATO produced in 1967, in the wake of France's withdrawal from the integrated command, the policy was defined as a combination of defence and détente. The aim now was not to eliminate the differences between East and West but to conduct the competition between the two systems in an orderly way. This picked up on the established Soviet concept of peaceful co-existence. A key principle in this was that there should be no

Alexander Dubcek (1921–92) had an orthodox Communist Party career in Czechoslovakia until he became general secretary of the party at the start of 1968 as the leader of a reforming faction. After the liberalization process was stopped in its tracks by the August invasion, he was taken to Moscow and forced to concede the end of his reforms. Although he remained party secretary until April 1969 he was pushed to the margins of national life. He returned to prominence when in December 1989 communist rule was overthrown.

overt interference in the internal affairs of the other bloc, hence the passivity over the crackdown in Czechoslovakia. Détente in this sense provided an argument for continued attention to defence as an insurance against any backsliding by the other side.

In Europe the diplomatic momentum behind détente was led by West Germany. Having been convinced as a result of the Berlin Wall that the Allies had no immediate interest in German unification, the Social Democrat government, led by Willy Brandt, who had been mayor of Berlin in 1961, pursued an 'ostpolitik'. This required convincing the East that West Germany

Czechs surge round Soviet tanks in August 1968. Many troops in the occupying force were quite bewildered as to why they were in Prague and why the population was so hostile. Joining in the invasion of 20 August were East German, Polish, Hungarian and Bulgarian forces. They faced more passive than active resistance, with communications disrupted to confuse them. Political life continued regardless until gradually, backed by Soviet power and with the reformers demoralized, the Czech hardliners seized control.

A remarkable photo, taken at Bratislava in the summer of 1968, when Dubcek hoped that he had secured a compromise whereby objections to his government would be removed in return for his assurances that communists would stay in control and Czechoslovakia would not leave the Warsaw Pact. Front row, from left to right: János Kádár (Hungary), Nikolai Podgorny (USSR), Alexei Kosygin (USSR), Fedor Shikov (Bulgaria), Ludvik Svoboda (Czechoslovakia), Leonid Brezhnev (USSR), Vladyslav Gomulka (Poland), Walter Ulbricht (East Germany), Alexander Dubcek (Czechoslovakia) and Mikhail Suslov (USSR). Suslov was the Soviet Politburo's leading ideologue.

The April 1974 'Revolution of the Flowers' in Portugal overthrew the government of Marcello Caetano, which had been in place since the dictator Salazar had been incapacitated with a stroke. It caused almost as many anxieties in Washington as the Czech revolution did in Moscow. No action was taken to reverse this revolution, however, and Western European socialist leaders worked hard to prevent Portugal from moving away from NATO.

was no longer revanchist or belligerent and that it was content to have normal relations with all communist states, including East Germany. Part of the thinking was that the extraordinary strength of the West German economy was in itself a critical form of power, more important than military strength, and that this power could be best exercised if the closest possible relations were allowed with the East. Critics worried about giving legitimacy to communist regimes and even reinforcing them through access to Western credits and technology. The *ostpolitik* led to a series of agreements that reinforced East–West links, including in 1969 a four-power agreement on Berlin that regularized the situation in the divided city.

As the 1970s progressed this economic strength of the two defeated powers of 1945 – Germany and Japan – appeared to count for more than the military strength of the victors. In 1973–4 came the oil shock, when Arab countries both established a link between access to oil and support for Israel and seized an opportunity to make a lot of money very quickly by suddenly raising the price of oil fourfold, with devastating effects on the international economy. Military strength appeared quite useless in the face of this political pressure and economic distress, but industrial strength offered a hope of survival. Russia, of course, was still judged at the time to be energy rich.

Vietnam had also left the Americans hesitant when it came to contemplating any new military commitments in the Third World. Rather than draw conclusions about the dangers of over-extension and massive intervention in local conflicts that they did not fully understand, the Russians looked to project their military power further afield. The last of the major Western empires to fall did so in 1974, as the Portuguese revolution led to an abrupt withdrawal from Portugal's colonies, providing opportunities for Soviet intervention, as did the overthrow of Haile Selassie in Ethiopia, plus various other disturbances, including, later in the decade, Afghanistan. These were often presented as being linked in some sort of grand strategy directed against the West's oil vulnerability.

The main cloud on the Soviet horizon was the tension with China. The risk that militant and reckless Chinese leaders might decide to pick a fight led to a massive build-up of forces in the Soviet Union's Far Eastern regions. Memories of being caught out by land invasions encouraged a determination never to show weakness to a potential enemy again. The urgent construction of a network of bases and supply lines in this distant region to support a military community manned and equipped to levels to match that facing NATO in Europe added to the domination of Soviet society by the defence sector. This included giving priority to heavy industry and putting the country's best brains to work on military projects. The general lack of productivity in the socialist command economy, combined with the devotion of up to a quarter of GDP to the non-productive defence sector, condemned the Soviet economy to years of stagnation while the West surged ahead. For the moment the economic consequences of

turning into a garrison state seemed less pressing to Brezhnev and his colleagues than the danger of two sets of enemies, to the East and to the West, teaming up together in a common cause against the Soviet Union. As there had been an apparently irretrievable breakdown in Sino-Soviet relations, Brezhnev had little choice but to compete for Washington's favours. In this he had reason to suppose that raw military strength gave him the stronger cards to play. By reinforcing détente with the West he could put a cap on Soviet military exertions in Europe and in nuclear weapons, gain recognition of equal superpower status, and possibly even bring about some trade and technology transfers that might help outweigh the economic costs of creating the military strength in the first place.

ARMS CONTROL

The first fruits of these attempts at arms control had come in 1972 with the Antiballistic Missile Treaty. The problems with taking strategic arms control much further lay with trying to put limits on offensive arms. ABM developments were faltering precisely because of the advances in offensive missile systems. Nor was there an agreed strategic concept to suggest how best to limit offensive weapons as there had been with the defensive ones. The best available was a political concept: parity, which basically required that the two sides demonstrate through agreement that they accepted an essential equality in capability. Unfortunately both sides had substantial nuclear inventories, similar in many

As the Soviet leadership watches atop Lenin's tomb, Soviet SS-11 missiles are driven through Red Square. By this time in the mid 1970s the SS-11, which had been the backbone of the Soviet ICBM forces for a decade, was being replaced by ICBMs with multiple warheads.

respects, but with important differences that rendered close comparisons difficult. Negotiations for almost two decades sought to develop credible measures that could create a contrived parity. MIRV technology constantly complicated this effort. In 1969, having taken the lead in deploying MIRVs, the Americans showed scant interest in control. Later the Soviet Union's larger missiles could individually accommodate more warheads.

Why should this matter? Recognition that mutual assured destruction might be a fact of life rather than a preferred strategy might have been expected to take the heat out of nuclear debate, for there seemed to be no way to reduce the risk of utter devastation to manageable proportions. None the less there was always reluctance to accept its logic. The move in weapons technology towards smaller and more accurate warheads opened up the possibility of a range of attack options, and not just an almighty assault against centres of civilization. There was, furthermore, a nagging worry that the Soviet Union did not accept the American line on assured destruction, that its whole instinct was to aim for victory in any combat, and that this aim could be discerned in doctrinal writing which never doubted that in a crisis the Soviet side would come off best.

Yet once the road to a first-strike capability was blocked, the risk of retaliation and escalation into all-out nuclear exchanges could never be removed. The effects of nuclear explosions on command-and-control systems and the enormous and rapid attrition of men and equipment made it very difficult to develop any sort of credible operational nuclear strategy. The most studied idea involved the Soviet Union mounting a partial first strike sufficient to obtain a strategic advantage even if not sufficient to deny a possibility for retaliation. This idea first made an appearance at the start of the 1970s and drove much American nuclear policy until well into the 1980s. The idea was that a surprise Soviet ICBM attack would knock out American ICBMs. Unable to retaliate in kind, now lacking accurate ICBMs, the president could only attack cities with the less accurate submarine-launched missiles. This would invite attack against American cities. It was assumed that an American president could be so dismayed by this situation that he would give up without any further effort.

There were many reasons to doubt this scenario. The Soviet leadership would have to be sure of the reliability and effectiveness of its missiles, certain that the Americans would neither simply launch their missiles at the first warning of an incoming attack nor respond as if this was really only about military targets when in fact it would leave millions dead. At any rate, it was not very difficult for the Americans to develop a response in kind. This was the origin of the Trident generation of submarine-launched ballistic missiles carrying many warheads, each with a high accuracy, while precision-guided cruise missiles were also developed for aircraft and submarines.

None the less, this scenario dominated discussions on strategic arms control in that it provided an explanation for the Soviet practice of constructing

extremely large ICBMs carrying many warheads with high explosive yields. In 1972, along with the ABM Treaty, the United States and the Soviet Union did agree to a five-year Interim Agreement on Offensive Arms which took the form of a 'freeze' on existing ICBM or SLBM (submarine-launched ballistic missile) launchers or those being prepared for deployment. The momentum at the time appeared to be with Moscow. From 1967 to 1972 the Soviet ICBM force grew from 570 to 1,406, while, even more dramatic, the SLBM force increased from 27 to 440, with more to come. As Russia was largely a continental rather than a maritime power, these systems had previously been assigned a much lower priority. The American lead in bombers and multiple warhead technology provided a degree of compensation, but over the next five years, as the Russians fitted multiple warheads to their much larger missiles, they drew well ahead on this measure as well.

In November 1974 President Ford (who had been propelled suddenly into office that year after Nixon resigned following the Watergate scandal) and Brezhnev met at Vladivostok and agreed a framework for an offensive arms treaty. This allowed for 2,400 delivery vehicles (bombers and missiles) for each side, of which 1,320 could be missiles with MIRVs. While both sides honoured these limits, which were not exactly restrictive, turning them into a treaty proved extremely difficult because of ambiguities over what should be included (such as

In November 1974 Gerald Ford, an accidental president following the successive resignations of Vice-President Spiro Agnew after allegations of corruption and then President Nixon as a result of the Watergate scandal, met with Brezhnev in Vladivostok. They agreed a framework agreement for a strategic arms treaty although it took until the presidency of Jimmy Carter for this to be turned into an actual treaty, and even he could not obtain Senate ratification.

US cruise missiles or Soviet systems based in Europe), and in part because of the decline of détente in the late 1970s.

The problems of agreeing parity at the nuclear level were nothing compared to those at the conventional level. The case that, in every sense that mattered, there was a basic equality in strategic systems was strong; this was not the case in conventional capabilities, where there was a clear imbalance against NATO. This point had been made through the simple 'bean count', through which two inventories were directly compared. As we have seen, this was the method normally used to see whether NATO had any chance of coping with a Warsaw Pact invasion. After McNamara's attempt in the early 1960s to argue that the

The British frigate HMS Leander *exercising in the 1970s off the coast of Scotland as part of NATO's Standing Naval Force Atlantic. Keeping open the Atlantic approaches was essential to NATO strategy to enable reinforcements from the United States to reach Europe in the event of war.*

conventional balance was not too bad, the failure to back flexible response with extra forces, and the Vietnam-induced decline in the self-confidence of not only American but Western armed forces in general, meant that few doubted that the trends favoured the Warsaw Pact countries. Ironically, only the Russians appeared to have taken seriously the call to prepare for an extended conventional battle.

At the start of the 1970s congressional hostility to the level of American military spending combined with irritation that the European allies were not carrying an appropriate share of the burden of military preparedness. This led to proposals, normally associated with the senior Democrat senator Mike Mansfield, for major cuts in the levels of American ground and air forces based in Europe. These were strongly resisted by President Nixon, not only because of the military consequences of allowing the Warsaw Pact an even greater superiority, but also because of the unfortunate political signal of potential abandonment that would be sent to the allies. Such a move threatened to destabilize the Atlantic alliance, obliging Europeans to consider defence arrangements other than dependence on the United States.

Кому мерещатся чужие территории,
Взглянуть полезно в зеркало истории!
С. Михалков. 1975

It might have been thought that Brezhnev would have delighted in this possibility. If the United States began to disengage from Europe, and if economic and political tensions loosened the ties that held the European members of NATO together, it might have been supposed that this could lead to a virtual Soviet hegemony. But Brezhnev could see dangers in this. The uncertainties created could deflect the new West German government away from thoughts of détente and instead towards a more assertive role, taking leadership of the NATO rump and engaging in rearmament to make up for America's lost support. He wanted a quiet life in Europe and so made a curious intervention in the debate surrounding congressional proposals for troop cuts. On the eve of one congressional vote in 1971 he made a speech agreeing to a long-standing but usually ignored NATO proposal for talks on reductions in conventional forces. Given the prospect of negotiated conventional disarmament, with Warsaw Pact numbers also brought down, Congress backed away from unilateral disarmament.

Actual talks – on Mutual Reductions in Forces and Armaments and Associated Measures in Central Europe (MFR for short) – began in 1973. There was no problem in defining what might constitute parity in this area: 900,000 air and ground troops on both sides with a sub-limit of 700,000 for ground troops. The problem was that there was no agreement on the starting point for the Warsaw Pact. NATO claimed a Warsaw Pact superiority of about 150,000 troops; Warsaw Pact data (acknowledged after the Cold War to have been knowingly false) conveniently showed virtual parity already. No progress was made.

THE REDISCOVERY OF THE OPERATIONAL ART

This was the background against which the American armed forces sought to rebuild themselves after Vietnam. The war had drained the army of confidence and credibility. There were plenty of indications of disarray and low morale. The move away from a conscript army may have removed a major source of political discontent among the young, especially those without the education and connections to obtain exemptions, but it did not improve the army. A military career held out few attractions, and to sustain their numbers the generals had to lower their standards for new recruits.

To revive the army the generals went back to basics. The most important war that they might have to fight would be against Warsaw Pact forces in Europe. This was the sort of campaign which they understood and for which it was possible to prepare and train. High-intensity war involved familiar forms of military organization and equipment, with none of the complex political demands of low-intensity conflicts. With this focus great strides were made during the first half of the 1970s in reviving the inner strength of the US Army.

It was, however, being prepared for a traditional battle – but did the army, or its political masters, understand what a traditional battle meant any more? In the mutual force reductions talks and elsewhere it was common to talk of a 'military balance', which simply compared numbers in standard categories – troops, tanks, artillery pieces, combat aircraft and so on. These provided little guidance on the actual outcomes of future combat, as could be readily illustrated by noting the numerical inferiority with which the Israelis habitually entered their wars. A proper 'dynamic' model of the military balance would need to crank in considerations of geography, alliance, mobilization, training, doctrine and so on, as well as equipment and manpower.

The basic problem for NATO in Europe lay in the speed with which reinforcements might be introduced from Soviet territory. American reinforcements would be on the other side of the Atlantic Ocean. If NATO's front-line force held out for more than a few days, communications across the Atlantic Ocean from the United States to Britain (as the main base from which operations would be mounted on the Continent) would have become as crucial as in the previous two world wars. Only by sea could sufficient men and equipment be moved. NATO placed great emphasis on anti-submarine warfare as the means of protecting shipping, enhancing the hazards facing the large

Soviet submarine fleet seeking to pass through the Greenland–Iceland–UK gap en route to the Atlantic. Attacks on NATO shipping might not have been a high priority for the Soviet Union, especially if the Soviet strategists assumed that the land war would be over before the sea war was decided. The first priority of the Soviet Navy would have been to protect the homeland from attack by NATO, including the submarine-based components of its nuclear deterrent. Although the Soviet Union built a substantial navy in the 1970s, helped by a formidable advocate in Admiral Gorshkov, it lacked the ports and overseas facilities to operate globally in an effective manner and never really got the hang of aircraft carriers.

The critical question, therefore, was whether a determined Warsaw Pact offensive could be held. Numbers and geography favoured the pact, and there was not even confidence in the West's technological edge as a form of compensation. While the Soviet Union might lag behind, it was often nimbler in turning new technologies into usable weapons systems. Furthermore, infatuation with advanced technology could result in a disregard of other critical features of military equipment including ruggedness, reliability and ease of operation – which the Soviet Union did not forget. Soviet designers, it was argued, built around the limitations of their troops and their industry while the West pushed them to their limits, with the result that the systems arrived late, well over cost, and were often difficult to operate effectively. In addition, there was a tremendous duplication of effort within NATO, as many countries had their own industries to protect and were not so sure of alliance that they wanted to become wholly dependent upon others for vital equipment.

The strength of the Warsaw Pact led serious commentators to wonder by the mid 1970s whether it could get itself into a position to launch an attack from a standing start – without warning – relying on its armoured divisions based in East Germany. If NATO was to cope it would need to be able to respond quickly to the first indicators of an enemy offensive. The problem was not warning time as such but the speed at which a political decision would be taken to mobilize. The indicators might be ambiguous. Diplomats might be concerned that any response would be a provocation, triggering the event that it was supposed to be preventing.

The success of 'smart' bombs in the 1972 Linebacker air campaigns in Vietnam combined with the October 1973 Yom Kippur War, which we shall discuss in the next chapter, drew attention to the potential of new weapons technologies. The early successes of Arab air defences in 1973 were notable, certainly when compared to the rout of the 1967 Six Day War, as was the growing prominence on the battlefield of accurate anti-tank munitions. As the combination of tanks and aircraft was normally considered the key to a successful offensive, and as these items were becoming increasingly expensive with each successive generation, the prospect that they could be picked out and destroyed at will by small and individually operated anti-tank and anti-aircraft

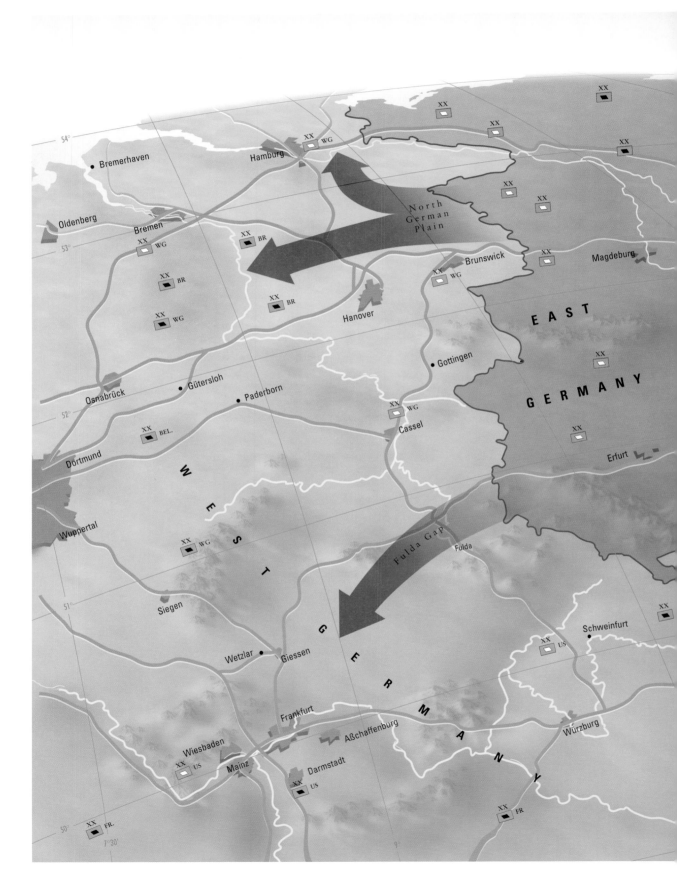

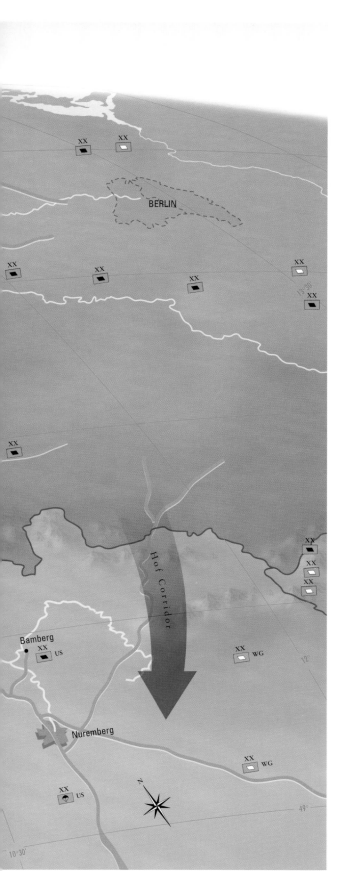

A bridge-laying armoured vehicle prepares to lay a 20m bridge capable of carrying tanks over a ravine during Warsaw Pact exercises in East Germany in 1981.

NATO versus Warsaw Pact

NATO troops were not optimally placed to prevent a major Warsaw Pact thrust through north Germany. Attempts to construct substantial, fortified barriers across the main invasion routes suffered from West German inhibitions about making the inner German border appear too permanent and memories of the ease with which the French Maginot Line was circumvented by advancing Germans in 1940. This map helps to explain why NATO was most worried about a fast-moving offensive through the Fulda Gap and why Hamburg appeared particularly vulnerable to a 'smash-and-grab' raid from the east.

Nato versus Warsaw pact
Northern Germany

XX ▭	armored division
XX ▭	motorized infantry division

weapons seemed to provide a boost for the defence, and by extension for NATO, an alliance committed to protecting the status quo.

The trend in opinion opposed to NATO's dependence upon the threat to use nuclear weapons first saw merit in developing more attractive conventional options. Those in the anti-nuclear movement, however, were wary about appearing to be committed to aggressive military postures. They were looking for a 'non-provocative' or 'defensive defence' – that is, a means of meeting a defensive objective, of protecting national territory, with unequivocally defensive means, able to absorb and frustrate an enemy offensive but not to undertake an offensive themselves. Ideas were developed in Germany and Scandinavia for popular militias armed with sophisticated but manageable precision-guided munitions. Such ideas were criticized on three grounds. First, popular militias of the sort required would not spring up spontaneously out of a modern urban society. To develop them would require a 'militarization' of the population that many of the advocates of the general approach would find abhorrent. Even professional troops would find it alarming to attempt to hold the line on fire-swept terrain. Second, the presumption was that the enemy objective was one of territorial occupation. Deterrence would be achieved by demonstrating that any occupation would be resisted at every stage. Unfortunately, this approach might not work so well against an enemy quite indifferent to the fate of the country and its people. Third, along with other proposals for reform, there was an exaggerated belief in the potential of new technologies.

While it is the case that those systems that make it possible to take the battle

into enemy territory are essential for an offence, the same systems can also be vital for an effective defence. Much depends on terrain and the tactical objectives of the moment. The standard calculation presupposed a rather static defence, with the enemy being forced to mount an effective attack and moving out into the open to prosecute it, thereby presenting lucrative targets to a grateful defender. Matters would rarely be so simple. Focusing on what a single missile could do to a tank or an aircraft or a ship ignored both the improving capacity of these targets to take evasive action or to effect counter-measures, and the vulnerability of those holding these weapons as they tried to identify and close in on their targets or simply lay in wait.

The operators would need to be in the right place at the right time. If this required any movement then the cover of protected positions would have to be relinquished and the risk of exposure to enemy fire accepted. That would argue for systems that could be protected by armour and with tracks to get over difficult terrain. Once a mobile anti-tank weapon is configured for mobility in a combat zone it soon begins to look suspiciously like a tank. Even in the Yom Kippur War the most effective anti-tank weapon turned out to be a tank.

Approaches based on attrition required the ability to concentrate firepower more effectively than the enemy. There were only a limited number of routes that the Warsaw Pact could follow in invading the West. The traditional approach to NATO strategy argued that by blocking these routes and mounting counter-attacks where possible, the enemy could be stopped and then pushed back. If this was not possible, then the nuclear option remained available. This

A simulated massed armour assault by Bulgarian and Hungarian T-54/55 tanks supported by Soviet Mi-24 helicopter gunships during the Shield '82 Warsaw Pact exercises on the Black Sea coast of Bulgaria.

traditional framework, still reflected in the US Army's 1976 Field Manual, was subjected to a series of challenges. First, the credibility of nuclear deterrence was coming increasingly to be doubted. The quality of conventional capabilities had to be judged on their own terms. Second, NATO forces were not as well organized for an active defence as they might have been. They were thinly spread and could be overwhelmed by a determined Soviet onslaught at any given point. The defence's advantages could be lost if it was out-ranged in artillery and if key positions were outflanked. NATO bases, a legacy of where the British and American armies ended up at the end of the Second World War, were not well located, resulting in a lack of defence in depth. There was particular concern about the development by the Warsaw Pact of the Operational Manoeuvre Group designed to penetrate behind enemy lines.

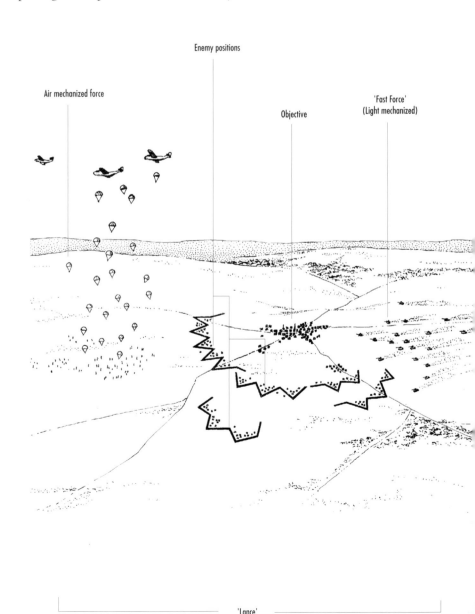

Enemy positions

Air mechanized force

Objective

'Fast Force'
(Light mechanized)

'Lance'

These concerns were picked up by a group who described themselves as military reformers. They developed a formidable critique of the current state of Western military thought and practice, and examined the possibilities for dramatic, high-speed operations and the search for the secret of the decisive battle. They argued for the rediscovery of the operational art which, it was claimed, was well understood by Soviet strategists but had been forgotten in the West, lost somewhere in the nether world between strategy and tactics. A series of imaginative operations, skilfully executed, could by itself determine the outcome of war. The reformers argued that not only had the East been building up its conventional forces more effectively than the West, but it also had a far better understanding of how to use them, and a much more advanced doctrine that was reflected in the organization and training of its forces.

From the reformers' perspective the military establishment of the United States appeared not only uninspired but also quite hopeless. Were the vast bureaucracies created to manage complex force structures and to procure sophisticated weapons systems capable of producing generals who understood strategy and were not wholly dependent

Main manoeuvre force

Mobile tank force

Heavy mechanized holding force

'Hammer'

'Dozer Blade'

OPERATIONAL MANOEUVRE GROUP

The Operational Manoeuvre Group (OMG) concept was designed to use tanks in an offensive mode, so that the attacking force could be compact enough to be truly manoeuvrable but powerful enough to be decisive. It involved a spearhead force of light tanks, possibly supported by paratroops or heliborne forces, making the first deep penetration. This would then be filled out using a mechanized division, bringing forward artillery in order to keep open the original axis and further develop the offensive.

upon technological fixes or influenced in every move largely by considerations of Washington politics? From an operational perspective US performance during the various limited conflicts in which it had been involved since 1945 was not impressive. The practical consequences of the lively debate on the conduct of non-nuclear warfare were initially limited. It came down to a competition between the advocates of manoeuvre and those of attrition through concentrated firepower. The situation was made more confusing by the association of the former with the proposals involved in a new US Field Manual and known as AirLand Battle, and of the latter with the Supreme Allied Commander, Europe, General Bernard Rogers, the 1976 version of the Field Manual and the study known as AirLand Battle 2000. Rogers wanted to develop long-range battlefield systems of high accuracy as 'deep-strike' weapons to disrupt follow-on enemy forces. There was also some argument for greater use of natural barriers and fortifications, though this was a politically sensitive matter within West Germany.

The reformers argued that if the operational art could only be revived, then NATO could move away from a simple reliance on attrition and towards greater awareness of the potential of manoeuvre. Their enthusiasm, and the poor performance of the US military in Vietnam, gained them many adherents. Not all the senior commanders were convinced, and the mockery to which they were subjected for their greater interest in management than in strategy probably did not help. The manoeuvre strategies advocated, they warned, had a certain air of unreality about them. They would be a high-risk option in European conditions, with Europe's urban sprawl and complex road and train networks, and would place enormous strains on good intelligence and effective command and control. A faulty manoeuvre could lead to absolute disaster and leave the rear exposed.

At any rate the most expensive items could not be procured in large numbers, and so the bulk of forces would be made up of more venerable and less futuristic systems. The forces were reluctant to sacrifice established capabilities by denying them sufficient ammunition, spares and training in favour of speculative R & D. There was a tension between the allure of high technology and the promise of high performance and the more mundane questions of reliability and serviceability. Military forces had been put together during the Cold War for purposes other than war-fighting. With the emphasis on deterrence and stability, as much was read into the disposition of the forces and their overall level as into their true combat readiness. There was a natural tendency to stress the teeth at the expense of the tail, measuring military strength in front-line forces rather than in airlift or sealift capabilities or ammunition stocks, and in the firepower of their weapons rather than their reliability or maintainability.

Alliance politics therefore limited the new

General Bernard Rogers was NATO's supreme allied commander, Europe (SACEUR) during the tense years of the late 1970s and early 1980s, when he sought to gear alliance strategy to meet the challenge of a Warsaw Pact strategy based on a quick offensive through NATO lines by the first echelon reinforced by a substantial second echelon.

conventional strategies. NATO military preparations reflected past compromises designed to keep certain allies on side or calm public opinion. The Germans in particular were sensitive to the political implications of any major recasting of NATO doctrine. They had committed themselves to NATO and rearmament on the basis of forward defence, which meant that they did not want to see their territory used to fight a manoeuvre campaign in depth. At the same time they were wary of extra 'fortifications', as these appeared too reminiscent of the Berlin Wall and attributed permanence to the inner German border, and distrusted ideas expressed in terms of 'deep strike', as that sounded too offensive-minded for a country that was trying to jettison its past aggressive image.

Even if all these limitations could have been eased, there were unavoidable uncertainties over the character and course of a third world war, of which the most obvious remained the possibility that sooner or later nuclear weapons would be used if one side made a decisive conventional breakthrough. Even with conventional weapons major uncertainties were developing. How well would the most advanced systems perform in battle out of test conditions? What would be the impact of measures designed to interfere with the electronic systems so critical to modern weapons and to surveillance and communication? Analyses of conventional military operations were becoming almost as unreal as analyses of nuclear operations.

The prospects for a future war appeared unappealing. There might be few opportunities to rest or hide. Weapon accuracy, improved sensors (capable of being used at night and through clouds) and the fact that equipment could be operated in all conditions meant that units were more likely to be found and, once exposed, to become vulnerable to fire. The combat zone was being

A rare example of an aircraft owned and operated by a number of nationalities. In the 1980s NATO introduced eighteen Airborne Warning and Control Systems (AWACS) aircraft to provide the core of the alliance's early-warning system.

extended with the range of weapons, adding to the number of potentially vulnerable targets, especially those whose location could be identified prior to the outbreak of hostilities. This would put a premium on dispersal and constant movement except for the most entrenched defences. Warfare under these conditions, even more than before, would be frightening, exhausting and confusing. Opportunities for sleep, replenishment and repair could be rare, which would put a premium on reliability and easy maintenance in weapon systems. This meant that the tempo would be faster and, as a result, the consumption of all consumables would be high, partly in response to the greater opportunities for employing firepower and the speed and intensity of combat. In the First World War some 65 tons of *matériel* were consumed each day by armies in the field. By the Second World War the figure was 675 tons. It had risen to 1,000 tons by Vietnam and 2,000 tons by the Yom Kippur War of October 1973. Yet the sophistication and cost of individual rounds of ammunition would mean that high consumption would be matched with low availability. Even more than before, the progress of any war that involved something more than a walkover

The Lance was a mobile field artillery tactical missile system that could deliver nuclear warheads out to a range of about 75 miles and conventional warheads to a range of about 45 miles. It first entered service with the US Army in 1973. It was bought by a number of NATO countries. Here West German troops prepare to launch a Lance during exercises.

would in part be determined by the speed with which *matériel* could be moved from the rear to the front and allocated to the units most in need. The quality of logistical arrangements would determine the capacity for mobility. Truly mobile units must travel light, fend for themselves over long periods and be able to repair key items of equipment. There was no evidence to suggest that this would be possible in a high-tempo war. There would also be a great dependence on command, control, communications and intelligence. The relevant systems were improving constantly here so there was the potential for a steady and possibly overwhelming stream of high-quality information. Yet the means of interfering with communications were also improving. So one moment a unit could be in regular touch with headquarters and the next moment cut off. There was little sense of how existing inventories, force structures and doctrines would interact in practice. Despite the use of the term 'conventional', there were no known 'conventions' available for guidance, for the new conventional weapons were far removed from those of the last world war, and their limited use in lesser conflicts was only moderately revealing.

The giant 89,600 ton American nuclear-powered aircraft carrier, USS Enterprise, *with a complement of up to 3,100 men and able to carry as many as eighty-five rotary and fixed-wing aircraft.*

CHAPTER SIX

THE LESSONS OF WAR

AS PAKISTANI RULE over its eastern territory comes to an end in December 1971, a former policeman is led away to prison in Dacca with a gun at his head held by a member of the Bengali Mukti Bahini militia. The origins of the war lay in West Pakistan's refusal to accept the victory of the separatist Awami League in the December 1970 East Pakistan elections. At the end of March 1971 civil war began, leading to the flight of up to 10 million refugees into India. India found the position intolerable and in December 1971 advanced to the East Pakistan capital, Dacca, and installed Sheikh Mujibur Rahman as the first prime minister of the People's Republic of Bangladesh.

THE LESSONS OF WAR

SOME GUIDANCE COULD BE obtained from the experience of post-war conflicts fought with conventional forces by countries apart from the two main blocs. For almost a quarter of a century the best evidence about the development of conventional warfare was dominated by series of wars between two sets of antagonists: the Indians and Pakistanis and the Arabs and Israelis. In both cases deep intercommunal conflicts influenced the manner in which the British retreated from their colonial responsibilities, and resulted in a legacy of continuing violence.

THE INDO-PAKISTANI WARS

In the case of the Indian Raj, prior to independence in 1947 relations between the Hindus and the Muslims were so bad that the new state had to be partitioned, with the Muslim areas becoming Pakistan. The origins of conflict lay in a dispute over the predominantly Islamic Kashmir, whose ruler was a Hindu and opted to join India. As a result there was a conflict between the two successor states – India and Pakistan – which resulted in fighting in 1947, 1965 and 1971, and periods of considerable tension thereafter. Pakistan was always the weaker party.

India concluded the original fighting over Kashmir in January 1949 by controlling the bulk of the territory, which it eventually annexed. It then found itself caught by the changing strategic context. Pakistan played the anti-Soviet card with the United States and joined the Baghdad Pact, obliging India to get closer to the Soviet Union. There were, however, limits to the extent to which India could play the Cold War game. Until the early 1960s the Soviet Union had to keep up the pretence of supporting China, which had a border dispute with India. In October 1962, at the time of the Cuban missile crisis, Chinese forces overran Indian positions on this border, exposing the weaknesses of the Indian Army, before unilaterally announcing a ceasefire and then withdrawing, holding on to some of the contested territory. In terms of military history this was an undistinguished episode, but in terms of Cold War history it was fateful.

When the fighting began, Moscow backed Beijing in an effort to shore up support in the communist world

Pakistani soldiers with vehicles left by the Indians after fighting in 1971. After the Indians invaded East Pakistan, Pakistan invaded Indian Kashmir. After minor gains the advance was soon halted.

behind its Caribbean policy. This annoyed India. When China started criticizing Moscow for its management of the missile crisis, retaliation took the form of greater sympathy for the Indian position. This failed to regain Delhi's affection but exacerbated the Sino-Soviet dispute. President Kennedy took the opportunity to repair relations with India, and started to provide military assistance. He had China in mind, although the move left Pakistan irritated. None the less, Pakistan was still sufficiently emboldened by India's weak performance in the battle with China to begin to assert itself along the disputed area of Karachi and also the virtually uninhabited Rann of Kutch. This led, in March 1965, to some fighting between the two, culminating in an inconclusive clash in August. Ominously for Pakistan, Indian forces were beginning to show the benefits of reform and extra expenditure. Equally significant, the conduct of the 1965 war worsened relations between the geographically separated eastern and western parts of Pakistan. The Bengali easterners had long felt discriminated against by the westerners and felt that they had been left in a vulnerable position by

Islamabad's anti-Indian activism. Tensions between the two sides grew to the point where there was an effective insurrection in 1970. Islamabad's repressive response to unrest resulted in immense hardship, leading to a flood of refugees into India – over 1 million from March to December 1970. India found the refugee flow a burden and this provided a pretext for starting to pick fights with Pakistani forces.

In November 1971 Indian forces began to move into East Pakistan. Pakistan tried to relieve the pressure by mounting diversionary air strikes, including some against Indian positions in Kashmir, followed by a ground offensive. This triggered a full-scale Indian invasion of East Pakistan by more than 160,000

Indian tanks, with their guns pointing into the bush countryside, advancing into Jessore, East Pakistan.

troops. They enveloped a Pakistani army less than half the size, disrupting communications and easily achieving air superiority. Soon the eastern capital of Dacca was under siege. On 16 December the Pakistani commander surrendered. The next day, with his counter-offensive in the West making no headway, Pakistani President Yahya Khan resigned. A new state – Bangladesh – was born. The war was over before the superpowers could do much about it. The Indians were none the less irritated by the presence of the US aircraft carrier USS *Enterprise* in the Indian Ocean, indicating at least the possibility of American assistance to Pakistan. One result of this was that in March 1974 India tested a 'peaceful' nuclear device, thereby reviving fears of the spread of nuclear

ABOVE: *The new state of Bangladesh was proclaimed on 16 December 1971, one of the few modern states to be clearly a creation of war. The chaotic and violent start to its existence was not auspicious. Attempts to control the population in Bangladesh, after months of upheavals, led to the establishment of what were called satellite towns, shown here. The first leader, Sheikh Mujibur Rahman, was assassinated in 1975, as was his successor in 1981.*

NUCLEAR PROLIFERATION

It is widely assumed that nuclear weapons must spread inexorably as they provide such obvious strategic advantages for the countries that have the know-how and resources to acquire them. The reality is more complex. A number of states have abandoned a nuclear option while many others have decided not to make the effort after having appeared quite keen to do so. Many of those who still wish to pursue the nuclear option are finding it difficult to do so. While states such as Iraq and North Korea cynically signed the Nuclear Non-Proliferation Treaty while trying to become nuclear powers, the treaty has been strengthened since 1990 and only a few countries now withhold their signatures.

Non-Proliferation Treaty
1990

signatories

non-signatories

weapons to Third World states, just a few years after the established nuclear powers (excluding China and with lukewarm French support) had ratified the Nuclear Non-Proliferation Treaty.

Events in the subcontinent were therefore of far greater significance for post-war international history than is often acknowledged. The Indian test led to a Pakistani nuclear programme, which was surprisingly successful, leaving the region with two antagonistic nuclear powers (both eventually tested devices in 1998) and the major issue dividing them – Kashmir – unresolved.

ARAB–ISRAELI CONFLICT

Britain had long struggled in Palestine to honour its obligations to the Jews to provide a national homeland while acknowledging the hostility of local Arabs to the influx of Jewish immigrants. After the Second World War the pressures became unbearable as Jews who had survived the Holocaust in Europe sought security in a country of their own. Britain found the policing requirements

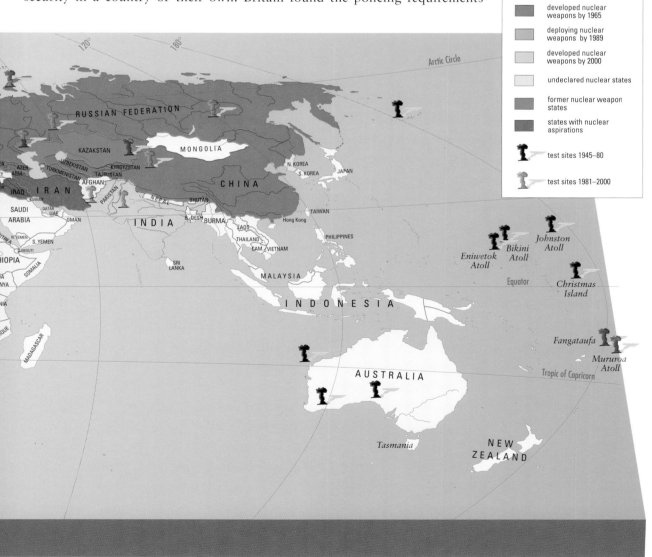

Spread of Nuclear Weapons
1945–2000

- developed nuclear weapons by 1965
- deploying nuclear weapons by 1989
- developed nuclear weapons by 2000
- undeclared nuclear states
- former nuclear weapon states
- states with nuclear aspirations
- test sites 1945–80
- test sites 1981–2000

In early November 1956 British troops parachute into Port Said. The pretext for this attempt to wrest control of the Suez Canal back from Nasser was found in the Israeli offensive against Egypt which had begun a few days earlier (in collusion with Britain and France). This led London and Paris to demand that both Israeli and Egyptian forces withdraw from the canal or they would intervene to enforce a cease-fire. Although they took the canal zone, international opposition, not least from the United States, forced their withdrawal by late December.

excessive and eventually gave up, handing the problem over to the United Nations, which, in a rare act of American and Soviet connivance, agreed independence for Israel in 1948. It was immediately attacked by over 30,000 Arab troops from five countries. The 15,000-strong Israeli force fought on three fronts, surviving through skilful leadership and determination against a force that did not enjoy high morale and was poorly led. By the time that the UN got the two sides to agree to an armistice in July 1949, Israel had expanded to take in much of the area that had been designated Arab lands.

The Arabs were loath to consider that the end of the matter. The origins of the next war, in 1956, lay in a belief by the Israeli government that a major show of force might oblige the Arab governments to acknowledge Israel's existence. In 1954 a military coup led by Gamal Abdel Nasser had overthrown the Egyptian monarch. Britain had then agreed to withdraw its force from the Suez Canal Zone, but as soon as this agreement was implemented, in June 1956, the Suez Canal Company, which controlled this vital waterway, was nationalized. This infuriated its joint owners, Britain and France. As diplomatic efforts failed to resolve the crisis, the two European powers colluded with Israel to decide the matter by military means. The intention was for Israel to attack Egypt, and then

Britain and France would use this as a pretext for retaking the Suez Canal Zone.

Israel faced little effective opposition as it moved across the Sinai to the Suez Canal. The British and French operation, however, was far less impressive. The logistics side was cumbersome and time-consuming. Eventually paratroopers landed at Port Said, but the blatant nature of the operation led the United States to put economic pressure on the Europeans to abandon it. Israel also had to withdraw, with a UN emergency force left to watch over the border with Egypt and supervise the Strait of Tiran which led to Israel's Red Sea port of Eilat. Instead of being crushed, Nasser emerged from the crisis as an Arab hero, with the colonialists humiliated and never able again to exert serious authority in the Middle East.

Nothing was settled, and for the next ten years the two sides prepared for another war. In May 1967 Nasser began to put pressure on Israel once again. By asking the UN force to leave, he indicated his readiness to blockade Israel. The rising tide of rhetoric in the Arab world, with intense discussions involving the front-line states of Egypt, Syria and Jordan, led Israel to conclude that it could not wait for a war to start on the Arabs' terms but must take the initiative. The Six Day War of June 1967 not only changed the politics of the Middle East but

SUEZ AND THE SINAI CAMPAIGN, 1956

Although there were some tough fights close to the border with Egypt, Israel's mastery of armoured warfare led to Egyptian forces having to choose between early withdrawal or later envelopment. By the time British and French paratroopers landed at Port Said, Israel had completed its campaign.

also encouraged a reappraisal of the art of warfare. The Israelis had already shown themselves in 1956 to be masters of armoured warfare. Now they showed themselves also to be masters of air power. On 5 June two hundred Israeli aircraft took off in complete radio silence against the main Egyptian air bases, intending to attack them from unexpected directions. The Egyptians were caught completely by surprise. By the time the senior commander realized what was going on, their air force no longer existed. In control of the skies, the Israelis pushed rapidly across the Sinai, stopping only at the Suez Canal.

Misled by Egyptian propaganda which denied the completeness of the Israeli air victory, and urged on by his people, King Hussein of Jordan entered the war. His forces put up a tough fight but they were soon forced out of the West Bank, including Jerusalem. With the momentum behind them, and ignoring for as long

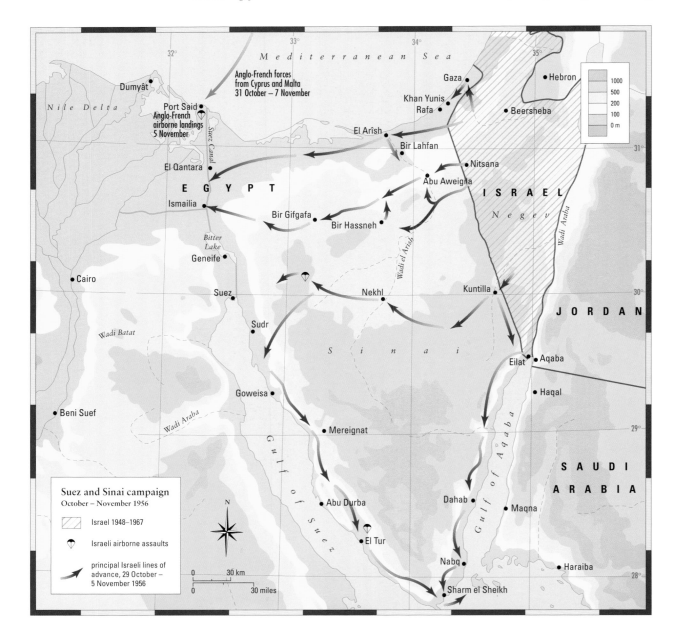

Suez and Sinai campaign
October – November 1956

Israel 1948–1967

Israeli airborne assaults

principal Israeli lines of advance, 29 October – 5 November 1956

as possible calls for a ceasefire, the Israelis took the Golan Heights from Syria, from where Israeli settlements had often been shelled. This time the Israelis refused to hand over any of the territory seized during the campaigns without a promise of full recognition and peaceful relations from the Arab governments, which the latter could not provide. Hostility towards Israel in the Arab world became more intense than ever. The difference now was that Israel had taken over territory occupied by large numbers of Palestinians, thereby creating an internal security problem.

Initially the Palestinian Arabs could do little to resist Israeli occupation. The Palestine Liberation Organization (PLO) turned, initially ineffectually, to guerrilla warfare and, more dramatically, to international terrorism to draw

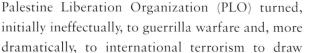

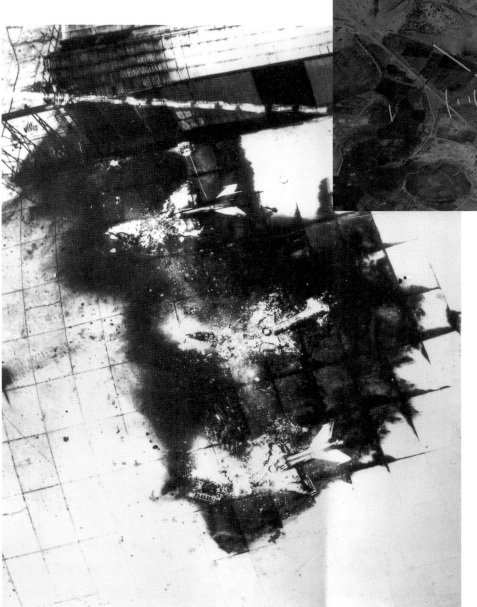

ABOVE: *A view through a Skyhawk bombsight at direct hits on Egyptian artillery positions in 1973.* LEFT: *In both 1967 and 1973 Israel was highly dependent upon its air force. In June 1967 these three Egyptian aircraft, with most of the others on the airfield, were destroyed before they had a chance to fly.*

attention to its cause. This campaign, and the Israeli reprisals that tended to follow individual operations, led to tensions within the Arab world. Jordan especially became annoyed with the increasing PLO presence, and King Hussein grew nervous about the PLO's influence. In September 1970 he took action against the PLO, which was expelled from Jordan.

There was some military action from 1969 to 1970 which became known as the war of attrition. Israel began to construct a defensive line (known as the Bar-Lev Line) along the Suez Canal. Egypt attempted to impede the construction by means of commando raids and artillery bombardments, which in turn led to Israeli air raids against targets such as airbases and anti-air-missile complexes. Nasser died in September 1970. His successor, Anwar Sadat, was even more of a gambler, but with a clearer strategy. He was prepared to go to war but with a

At an Arab summit conference in 1957 Egyptian President Gamal Abdel Nasser stands with King Saud of Saudi Arabia and President Shukri El-Kewalty of Syria to his right and the young King Hussein of Jordan to his left.

political purpose. He did not expect to defeat Israel but to shock it into negotiations. Meanwhile he saw improved links with the United States, and by extension a diminution of those with the Soviet Union, as essential to making the negotiations work. Only Washington could act as a mediator. Arab planning this time was much more careful. Israel noticed Syrian and Egyptian preparations, but did not accept until too late that they were serious. For once the Arabs achieved the advantage of surprise.

On 6 October, the Jewish Day of Atonement (Yom Kippur), Egyptian forces crossed the Suez Canal in a well-executed operation while the Syrians pushed across the Golan Heights. Fortunately for Israel the Egyptians, nervous about getting too far from their defensive cover, did not press home their immediate advantage. The Israelis needed the time to cope with the Syrian offensive, which was gaining ground and could only be stopped by the Israeli Air Force accepting that it could not take the normal first step of eliminating the Syrian Air Force and Syria's air defences. Eventually the Syrians were pushed back and even chased to within 20 miles of Damascus. Stung by accusations that they were letting the Syrians down, a week after obtaining the bridgehead on the eastern side of the canal, Egyptian forces began to move towards the mountain passes through the Sinai. The Israelis not only soon blocked the Egyptian advance but managed to get a tank unit between the Arab armies. This crossed the canal on

In October 1973 the Egyptians sought to wipe out the humiliation of 1967 by retaking the Suez Canal. Here Egyptian soldiers and equipment move across one of eleven pontoon bridges over the canal. Later nine of these bridges were destroyed by the Israelis.

16 October, and the next day was followed by an army brigade. Soon the Egyptian Third Army was surrounded. Only extensive American diplomacy extracted it.

Although this was another military defeat for Egypt, it was more of a political victory. As Sadat had intended, Israel was shocked by the effort and the loss of 2,500 men, more than three times the number lost in June 1967 and

President Jimmy Carter's substantial diplomatic achievement was to forge a peace treaty between President Anwar Sadat of Egypt and Prime Minister Menachem Begin of Israel. Begin (1913–92) had been a member of the Irgun which used terrorism to force Britain to grant independence and went on to lead the Israeli right-wing, promoting Jewish settlements in the occupied territories, so he was somewhat surprised to win the Nobel Peace Prize in 1978. His premiership was broken by the ill-fated invasion of Lebanon in 1983. Sadat (1918–81) also had a hard-line past as a member of Nasser's group that took power in 1954. He succeeded Nasser as Egyptian president in 1970. He gained in stature among Arabs for launching war against Israel in 1973 but became more controversial when he made his historic visit to Israel in 1977, leading to the 1978 Camp David Accords. In 1981 he was assassinated by Muslim extremists while reviewing a military parade.

against losses for Syria and Egypt of about 8,000 each. Both sides lost half their tanks. Egypt and Syria lost 250 aircraft out of about 800; Israel 115 out of 500. The early Israeli desperation, and the need for massive resupply of war *matériel*, was used by Washington to remind Israel of its dependence, while the later Arab desperation was used to develop close links with the Arab capitals as Henry Kissinger arranged the separation of forces in some hectic shuttle diplomacy. In 1975 Sadat entered into a formal agreement with Israel to regain control of the useful parts of the Sinai and to enable the Suez Canal to be reopened. In 1977, in a dramatic gesture, he invited himself to Israel and set in motion a peace process which concluded with the 1978 'Camp David' agreements. This led to diplomatic relations between Egypt and Israel but, because the latter had been unyielding on the question of the West Bank, other Arabs considered it a sell-out and Egypt was left isolated.

Thus the cost of a peace deal, which removed a real strategic threat to Israel, was the further radicalization of the Palestinians. Instead of the PLO's guerrilla campaign allowing them to push into the occupied territories, they found themselves pushed back into neighbouring territory, and in particular Lebanon, already a country deeply divided among Christians and Muslims. The more raids that were mounted from Lebanon, the more Israeli reprisals. Eventually the country erupted into a civil war which drew in both Syria and Israel. Israelis lent their support to the Christian Phalangists, who were concerned about the

increasingly influential role of the PLO in Lebanon. In March 1978 the Israelis invaded with some 20,000 troops. They left in return for a UN peacekeeping force acting as a buffer between Israel and Lebanon. The UN was unsuccessful in this role, and in June 1982 Israeli forces moved into Lebanon, pushing the UN forces aside. The invasion soon moved beyond the initial objective of a limited security zone and aimed to expel the PLO from Lebanon. To give it a free run to Beirut, Israel moved to destroy Syrian air defences in the Bekaa Valley (by getting the defenders to turn on their radars using decoys so that their positions could be pinpointed and then attacked) and defeated Syrian armour in a battle. Israeli forces encircled Beirut, trapping 7,000 PLO fighters, who were allowed to leave the country peacefully in September.

The murder of President-elect Bashir Gemayel ruined the chances for internal peace within Lebanon. As a reprisal Christians massacred Palestinians in the refugee camps at Sabra and Chatilah. The Israelis failed to prevent this. This led the United States to become directly involved. Initially this was to help keep the peace, but it saw an opportunity to make a wider breakthrough and sponsored an agreement in May 1983 envisaging Israeli withdrawal from Lebanon in return for the normalization of relations between the two countries. As that depended on local Islamic and Syrian compliance it was always ambitious. The result was further civil war in which the United States found itself caught and of which the peace deal was a casualty. In October 241 US marines were killed by a suicide

For Israel the most important moment of the 1967 war had been the capture of East Jerusalem, from which Jews had been excluded since 1948. This set up yet another stumbling block to a final peace accord.

Sunday 23 October 1983 became infamous for the death of some 241 US marines when their barracks in Beirut was rammed by a suicide bomber in a truck laden with explosives. Less well remembered is the simultaneous attack by the same method on the headquarters of the French force, which led to twenty-seven deaths. Here French soldiers sift through the rubble.

ISRAEL IN LEBANON

In 1978 a UN force was placed along the border to discourage Palestinian raids against Israel and Israeli incursions into Lebanon. It was swept aside in 1982 when Israeli forces moved into southern Lebanon, initially to clear the border areas of Palestinian fighters. The ease of the early advances tempted the Israelis into pushing the PLO out of Lebanon altogether and moved into Beirut. The PLO forces agreed to leave Beirut with guarantees for their own safety and that of their civilian dependants. Once Israeli troops occupied West Beirut, however, the Christian Phalangists massacred hundreds of Palestinian civilians in the refugee camps at Sabra and Chatilah.

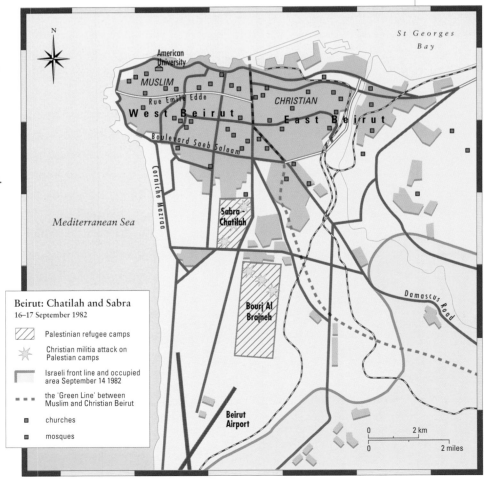

Beirut: Chatilah and Sabra
16–17 September 1982

⬚⬚⬚ Palestinian refugee camps

✳ Christian militia attack on Palestian camps

▬ Israeli front line and occupied area September 14 1982

– – – the 'Green Line' between Muslim and Christian Beirut

▪ churches

▪ mosques

St Georges Bay

American University

MUSLIM

Rue Emile Edde

CHRISTIAN

West Beirut **East Beirut**

Boulevard Saeb Salaam

Corniche Mazraa

Mediterranean Sea

Sabra - Chatilah

Bourj Al Brajneh

Damascus Road

Beirut Airport

0   2 km
0   2 miles

bomber in a truck who drove at their barracks. French troops, also part of a multinational peacekeeping force, were killed at the same time. The next February the multinational force withdrew. Israel's forces continued to occupy southern Lebanon, working with a Christian militia. As the Iranian-backed Hizbollah group grew in strength, Israel found this occupation painful to sustain (although it hung on until 1999).

The Arab–Israeli wars were studied avidly by the armed forces of other nations, in part because they pitted the Warsaw Pact against Western equipment. That the Israelis normally won such contests could be put down as much to superior training, doctrine and morale, although the technological edge made a

OVERLEAF: *The Israeli shelling of West Beirut, August 1982. This led to the evacuation of some 11,000 Palestinian fighters.*

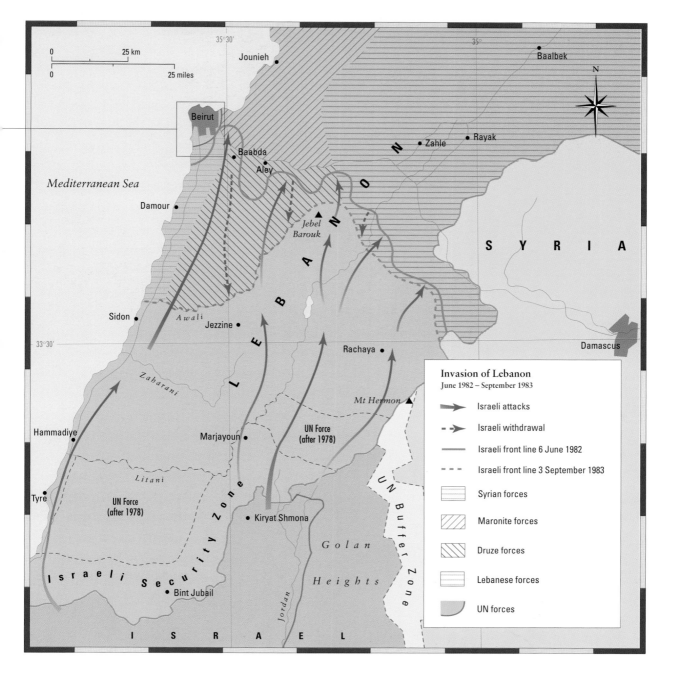

Invasion of Lebanon
June 1982 – September 1983

→ Israeli attacks

- ‑ ‑> Israeli withdrawal

—— Israeli front line 6 June 1982

- - - Israeli front line 3 September 1983

Syrian forces

Maronite forces

Druze forces

Lebanese forces

UN forces

difference. Israel's most potent weapon was its air force, and this made the decisive difference in all its campaigns and brought home to all observers the importance of gaining command of the air, if necessary through pre-emptive attack – a potentially destabilizing message for other conflicts. The 1973 war also introduced a wider public to the new smart weaponry, and the apparent vulnerability of large and expensive military assets to relatively portable guided

From the mid 1980s the Israelis attempted to build up the largely Christian, 17,000-strong Southern Lebanese Army as a means of controlling the area adjacent to Israel's northern borders. The militia proved unable to suppress the militant Islamic Hizbollah.

weapons. For most professional observers the big lesson to be drawn from October 1973 was the fluidity, tempo and intensity of contemporary war, which suggested that concepts based on holding a line and imposing attrition on the enemy were outdated.

This conclusion may have had some validity for a conventional battle involving substantial and reasonably advanced forces. It might have been argued that events in Lebanon warned of different sorts of dangers, of terrorist attacks and complex, vicious intercommunal conflicts in which sensitivity to the local political situation, backed by troops on the ground, was often as important as firepower, especially when dependent upon aircraft. Even for those interested in regular warfare between two states, the most striking feature of the wars of the 1980s was how reminiscent they were of those of previous generations, illustrating how factors of geography and politics intersect with those of force structure and doctrine. In terms of the impact on Western perceptions of future war the most important conflict was the Falklands War of 1982, largely because it directly involved a leading NATO country. The most substantial war of all was that between Iraq and Iran, lasting longer than either world war, causing millions of casualties and even seeing the use of chemical weapons and missile attacks against cities. Few military lessons could be drawn in terms of Western military practice, except that there was an indication of how Western armed forces might influence the course of another's conflict.

On 5 September 1972 eight members of the Palestinian Black September group, armed with Kalashnikovs and hand grenades, broke into the Olympic Village at Munich. In exchange for ten Israeli hostages still alive, the Arabs asked for the release of 256 prisoners. While the Olympic Games continued it was arranged that they would be flown out with the hostages to an Arab country. As they were being transferred to the aircraft German police opened fire. The terrorists were killed but so were hostages as grenades were lobbed into their helicopters. In all eleven Israeli athletes were killed. Here a hooded terrorist stands on the balcony of the Israeli athletes' apartment.

ANTI-TANK WEAPONS

The anti-tank weapons that can be carried by the infantry have shown growing power and accuracy. Anti-clockwise from the right, the anti-tank weapons illustrated here are a Second World War 2.75-inch anti-tank rocket launcher 'Bazooka'; a US M47 'Dragon' optically tracked wire-guided system with infra-red missile tracking; a US 66mm M72 A2 single-shot throw-away rocket launcher; and a US 3.5-inch M20 'Super Bazooka' rocket launcher.

ANTI-TANK ROCKET
LAUNCHER 'BAZOOKA'

'SUPER BAZOOKA'
ROCKET LAUNCHER

SINGLE-SHOT
ROCKET LAUNCHER

OPTICALLY TRACKED
WIRE-GUIDED SYSTEM

THE FALKLANDS WAR

Argentina had long held that the Falkland Islands, a few hundred miles from its coast, had been unjustly seized by Britain in 1833. By 1982 the population of the colony was under 1,800 and slowly declining, as was the local economy. However, the islanders were hostile to any transfer of sovereignty to Argentina, and British governments respected their right to self-determination, though little was done to protect the islands. After a curious incident involving Argentine scrap-metal merchants landing illegally on the dependency of South Georgia, which led to Britain preparing to eject them, the Argentine junta decided to bring forward

SEA HARRIERS

Although the landing of British forces at Port San Carlos was unopposed the Argentine air force was still intact and it caused considerable damage. The demonstrated superiority of the Royal Navy's Sea Harriers, equipped with American Sidewinder missiles, inhibited Argentine pilots. When Argentine aircraft were forced by the Harriers to turn back rather than engage it led to severe losses amongst those aircraft that failed to do so – some twenty-six were brought down by Harriers during the course of the conflict.

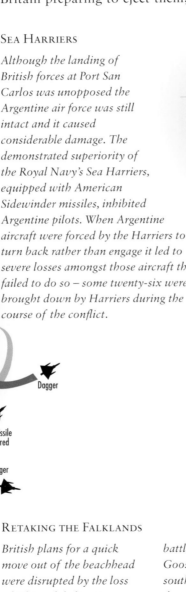

incoming
attack

Dagger

missile
fired

Dagger

missile
fired

Sea Harrier
patrol

Jason Islands

King George
Bay

Weddell
Island

Queen Charlotte
Bay

Weddell
Settlement

Port Stephens ●
Settlement

70°30'

70°

60°30'

RETAKING THE FALKLANDS

British plans for a quick move out of the beachhead were disrupted by the loss of Chinook helicopters when the Atlantic Conveyor *was sunk. This meant that Three Commando Brigade had to walk to Stanley on the northern route. After the*

battle for Goose Green the southern route was developed by Five Infantry Brigade. The Argentine garrison defending Stanley supposed this to be the main British attack, which they assumed to have

been disrupted significantly by the casualties caused by the air attack on HMS Sir Galahad.

plans for the invasion of the Falklands, which were successfully implemented on 2 April, resisted by a small detachment of Royal Marines. With impressive speed Britain responded by sending a large task force to the South Atlantic, including two aircraft carriers and, eventually, some 28,000 servicemen. Part of the purpose was to back a diplomatic initiative led by the United States. This failed.

On 25 April British forces retook South Georgia. At the start of May British Harrier aircraft began to strike Argentine positions, including the runway at Stanley, the capital. The attempt to draw out Argentine air and naval forces achieved limited success, but did lead to the sinking of the Argentine cruiser, the

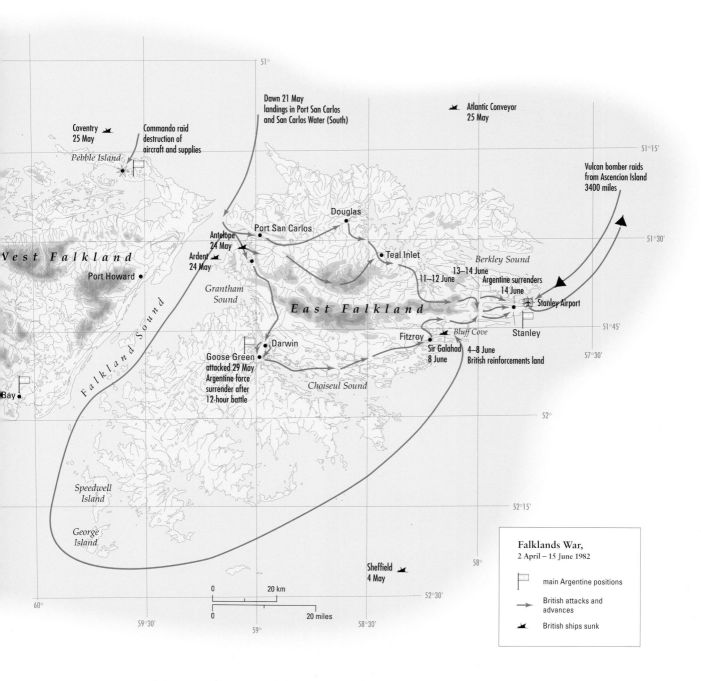

Coventry
25 May

Commando raid
destruction of
aircraft and supplies

Pebble Island

Dawn 21 May
landings in Port San Carlos
and San Carlos Water (South)

Atlantic Conveyor
25 May

Vulcan bomber raids
from Ascencion Island
3400 miles

Douglas

Port San Carlos

Antelope
24 May

West Falkland

Ardent
24 May

Port Howard

Teal Inlet

Berkley Sound

13–14 June

11–12 June

Argentine surrenders
14 June

Grantham
Sound

East Falkland

Stanley Airport

Stanley

Bluff Cove

Fitzroy

Sir Galahad
8 June

4–8 June
British reinforcements land

Darwin

Goose Green
attacked 29 May
Argentine force
surrender after
12-hour battle

Choiseul Sound

Bay

Speedwell
Island

George
Island

Sheffield
4 May

0   20 km

0   20 miles

Falklands War,
2 April – 15 June 1982

main Argentine positions

British attacks and
advances

British ships sunk

General Belgrano, by a nuclear submarine with the loss of 360 lives. This discouraged the Argentine fleet from leaving port thereafter, but was followed by the sinking of a British destroyer, HMS *Sheffield*, by means of an air-launched Exocet missile. More unsuccessful diplomatic activity, this time led by the UN, preceded the amphibious landing of British forces on 21 May at Port San Carlos. As troops struggled to establish themselves ashore, there were days of air raids against the British ships. Many Argentine aircraft were shot down, but three British warships were sunk and, crucially, one merchant ship, the *Atlantic Conveyor*, with the loss of a number of helicopters. On 28 May 600 British troops defeated a larger Argentine garrison at Goose Green, after heavy fighting, and then moved towards the main Argentine garrison based in and around Stanley. An attempt to move troops by sea ended in disaster on 8 June when the troopship *Sir Galahad* was caught by Argentine aircraft. Argentine land resistance was serious in places, although poorly organized, and was worn down through combinations of bombardment and infantry attacks. On 14 June the Argentine garrison surrendered and soon the Argentine junta had collapsed.

Because of the distances the amount of air power involved was limited. Using two small carriers with Harrier jump-jets, Britain had just enough air cover. The role of modern smart weapons was underlined by the impact of a few French Exocet anti-ship missiles, bringing home the vulnerability of surface ships to air and submarine attacks. The most important lessons from the Falklands, however, related to the traditional military concerns of having well-trained and motivated

HMS Antelope *sinks in Port San Carlos Water, May 1982.* Antelope *had been hit by Argentine bombs which had failed to explode.*

After the Argentine garrison at Stanley surrendered on 14 June 1982, prisoners are gathered together. By sending so many troops to the Falklands the Argentine commanders had created a great logistical problem for themselves. By the time of the surrender most soldiers were cold and hungry.

troops, and the vital importance of logistics. The most important British feat was to sustain a task force over 8,000 miles from home. Argentina's most significant failing was in not disrupting this extended supply line more than it did, and in not stopping its own connections with its garrison on the islands being disrupted.

THE IRAN–IRAQ WAR

The Iran–Iraq War began on the night of 21–22 September 1980 when Iraqi President Saddam Hussein sought to take advantage of the tumult within Iran following the overthrow of the shah. At a minimum, his objectives were to blunt the perceived ideological challenge posed by the new Iranian regime and to reverse the 1975 Algiers agreement between the two countries on the 120-mile Shatt-Al-Arab waterway, which provided Iraq with its primary access to the sea. The initial Iraqi offensives made very extensive inroads into Iranian territory. However, by November 1980 the offensive had run its course. In September 1981 Iranian counter-attacks began. Although throughout the war Iraq held significant parts of Iranian territory, by the end of 1982 the Iranians had also begun to make some inroads into Iraqi territory. Through this period, Iran continued to pressurize Iraq, with its offensives culminating in the taking of the Fao Peninsula in February 1986 as part of a move towards the city of Basra. Iraqi forces were also held down from 1984 by a Kurdish insurgency in northern Iraq.

At the end of 1978 the shah of Iran was overthrown in the face of a popular uprising. Here youths try to topple over a statue of the shah of Iran in Tehran while holding up a portrait of the leader of the Islamic opposition, Ayatollah Khomeini.

The Iranians had three times the population (45 million as against 14 million) and were stronger on land. The Iraqis were stronger in the air, especially from 1984, and also had more surface-to-surface missiles. Though both sides were dependent upon oil for revenues, only a small proportion of Iraqi oil went by sea, whereas the greater part of Iranian oil went by this route. The Iranians, therefore, had a greater stake in keeping the Straits of Hormuz open and had no reason to encourage a 'tanker war'. All this explains why Iraq responded to its weakness in the land war through escalation as part of an attempt to internationalize the conflict. This included the 'tanker war', as the Iraqis attacked ships exporting Iranian oil, which began in February 1984. The use of chemical weapons against Iranian troops was first reported in late 1983, and Iraqi strategic strikes against Iranian population centres with aircraft and missiles began in 1985.

By maximizing international pressure on Iran to withdraw to pre-war boundaries, Iraq accepted that the Iranian territory which it continued to hold was less important than the Iraqi territory which Iran now held. Diplomatically Iraq encouraged UN resolutions which allowed for a return to the status quo ante

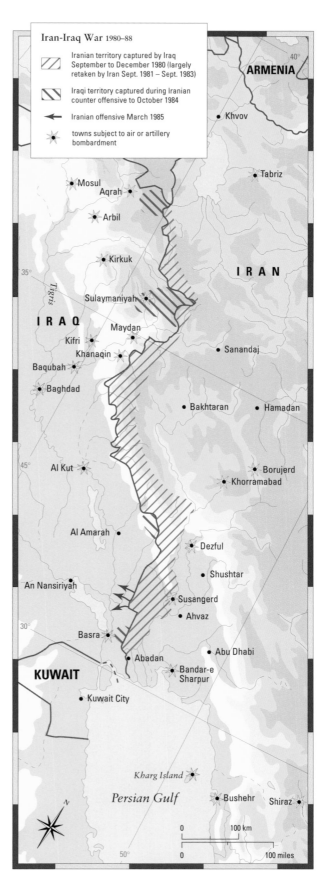

Iran-Iraq War 1980–88

Iranian territory captured by Iraq September to December 1980 (largely retaken by Iran Sept. 1981 – Sept. 1983)

Iraqi territory captured during Iranian counter offensive to October 1984

Iranian offensive March 1985

towns subject to air or artillery bombardment

THE IRAN–IRAQ WAR

The Iran–Iraq War was unusually vicious. Initial Iraqi gains were followed by successful Iranian counter-attacks, leading to a stalemate. Successive Iranian offensives met with dogged Iraqi resistance, on occasion helped by chemical weapons. Unable to win on land Iraq tried to put pressure on Iran by attacking its cities with missiles and attempting to choke off its oil trade by attacking shipping in the Gulf. Iran had managed to isolate itself so effectively from international support that it was obliged eventually to agree to a ceasefire in April 1988.

bellum, while avoiding condemnation of Iraqi aggression, and urged the major powers, especially the United States, to take actions that would oblige Iran to comply with these resolutions. The Americans took up the Iraqi case to an extent surprising in the light of Iraq's radical past and recent behaviour, including responsibility for the initial aggression, but more comprehensible given the American dislike of Iran.

In the 1970s Iran had been closely associated with the United States and Iraq with the Soviet Union. As Iranian revenues grew with the price of oil, the shah had spent hugely on Iran's armed forces, and all the Western powers had been happy to oblige him by selling arms, failing to notice the unrest developing within the population, which was not seeing its share of the oil wealth. After the

overthrow of the shah at the end of 1978, however, a crisis in US–Iranian relations developed, leading to the 1979–81 hostage crisis and the rupture of diplomatic relations. The hostage crisis was deeply embarrassing for the United States, and contributed to the defeat of Jimmy Carter as president in 1980. Sixty-six hostages were seized by students who had been demonstrating outside the American embassy, angry at what they perceived to be twenty-five years of US exploitation of the country and support of a dictatorship. The Iranian government refused to take steps to get them released. An American attempt to mount a rescue mission using helicopters to reach Tehran failed disastrously when the helicopters crashed, with President Carter's apparent attempt to micro-manage the mission adding to the political damage. The Iranians had waited until the day Carter left

During the war with Iran, Iraq resorted a number of times to chemical weapons to repel Iranian troops. At the same time they were used against disaffected Kurds, notably after the war against civilians at Halabjah.

office to release the hostages, but the new Reagan administration shared the antipathy to Iran, as did the Arab Gulf states, fearful of the threat posed by Islamic fundamentalism to their conservative monarchies.

Like China in the 1960s the new Iran was not playing a Cold War game. While Moscow saw an opportunity to establish some influence in Tehran, the new Islamic regime, led by the Ayatollah Khomeini, had no intention of getting close to those who were suppressing an Islamic revolt in Afghanistan. None the less the Soviet Union's attempt to ingratiate itself with Iran was sufficiently alarming for Iraq, and the need for technical support and advanced arms so pressing, to give the West an opportunity to wean it away from Soviet influence. France had long been working on improved relations with Baghdad – it was the largest arms supplier after the Soviet Union – and now the United States began to explore the possibility of re-establishing diplomatic relations with Iraq. It steadily expanded its contacts, offered credits and technologies, while at the same time, with 'Operation Staunch', it worked to prevent new weapons getting to Iran. At the end of 1984 diplomatic relations were restored.

Yet in terms of size and geography Iran was strategically more important, and some in the Reagan administration wondered whether the pro-Iraqi tilt had gone too far. In late 1986 it was revealed that, in contradiction to official policy, members of the National Security Council staff had established links with senior Iranian officials and arranged for the transfer of some weapons. The objective of this was to secure the release of American hostages held by radical groups in Lebanon and, latterly, to acquire funds which could be channelled to the anti-government 'Contra' rebels in Nicaragua. Despite a hope that the transfer of weapons might strengthen 'moderates' in Tehran, the venture produced no serious concession from Iran and the resulting scandal caused immense political damage to the Reagan administration, and encouraged, by way of compensation, a further tilt in Iraq's direction.

Iraqi oil was exported largely via land pipelines, so if Iran was to retaliate for Iraqi attacks on tankers that affected its oil exports, then Iraq's apparent ally, Kuwait, provided the next best target. During 1987 the United States agreed to reflag and so protect Kuwaiti tankers, in part because if it had not done so the Russians would have picked up the task. On 17 May 1987, just before this operation began, two Exocet missiles from an Iraqi F-1 fighter struck USS *Stark*, then 70 miles north of Bahrain. Thirty-seven crewmen were killed. Not only was Iraq forgiven after it apologized, but Washington decided to build up American naval strength in the Gulf to forty-one ships. Unfortunately, on one of the first convoys a vintage mine hit the reflagged supertanker *Bridgeton*, which was triply embarrassing to the United States: by indicating that reflagging did not guarantee American protection; by ending with the crippled tanker protecting the warships, which were much more vulnerable to mines; and by revealing that the United States lacked a modern mine-sweeping capability.

Pressure on Iran was sustained through the UN Security Council Resolution

598 of July 1987, which demanded an immediate ceasefire and withdrawal to 'internationally recognized boundaries'. It was assumed that as this meant Iran relinquishing its main bargaining card without any definite settlement it would be reluctant to comply, in which case the Americans were ready to push for mandatory sanctions against Iran. This did not quite go to plan, as Iran was more responsive than expected and the rest of the Security Council more cautious. Frustrated, in August Iraq revived the tanker war, and then, at the end of February 1988, the war of the cities. Around 170 Scud-B missiles rained down on Tehran and other Iranian cities, causing many casualties and mass evacuations. Iran responded with thirty-five to forty Scud strikes.

The cumulative pressure was now telling on Iran. Another mine incident on a US warship in April led to American attacks against an oil platform allegedly linked with the mining operations, followed by an unequal fight between the American and Iranian navies. Iran's navy consisted of a few frigates and corvettes, eight fast-attack craft and some thirty to fifty speedboats with small arms and anti-tank rockets. The United States sank or crippled six Iranian ships. This was as Iraq was retaking the Fao Peninsula. The sense of weakness and isolation undermined Iran. On 3 July the USS *Vincennes* shot down an Iranian Airbus, killing 290 Iranian civilians. This tragic incident appears to have knocked

One of the more curious episodes during the Iran–Iraq War came when an Iraqi aircraft fired two Exocets at a US guided missile frigate, USS Stark, which was part of an American force ostensibly there to prevent Iran shutting off the Straits of Hormuz. Considerable damage was caused and thirty-seven American sailors were killed. Washington accepted an apology from Saddam Hussein, although there remain suspicions that the attack was intentional, as part of Saddam's strategy for internationalizing the war.

THE STINGER

Designed to replace the first lightweight surface-to-air missile, the Redeye, the Stinger came into service with the USA in the early 1980s. It is a man-portable, shoulder-fired guided missile system which allows the operator to engage low-altitude jet, propeller-driven and helicopter aircraft. It uses a passive infrared seeker to find the target.

A Soviet MIL 24D helicopter gunship against the background of a wintry Kabul. These became one of the main instruments for keeping up pressure against the rebel Afghan Mujaheddin.

Iranian confidence, already at a low point, and soon afterwards a ceasefire was agreed.

There were no lessons for Cold War armies in the tactical conduct of the Iran–Iraq War, except that certain regimes, once they got into a war, were prepared to squander manpower. It was revealing in indicating how these conflicts could be internationalized, in terms of support for the financing of the war effort, provision of equipment and supplies, and even, as with the maritime operations in the Gulf, how a limited intervention by modern units could make a substantial difference. The international dimension to the war showed the continuing influence of Cold War considerations, but also indicated how fluid politics was starting to become. In the end both the United States and the Soviet Union were backing Iraq – or, more accurately, opposing Iran.

AFGHANISTAN

Not long after the Iranian revolution, in December 1979, the Soviet Union invaded Afghanistan. The origins of this intervention lay in a coup in Kabul in April 1978 led by communist officers. The new regime found its secular ideology very difficult to impose in a deeply Islamic country, and soon floundered in the face of guerrilla warfare by Islamic rebels (Mujaheddin). Moscow became

AFGHANISTAN

The actions of the Russians in Afghanistan suggested that they had learned nothing from the Americans in Vietnam. Again it was rebels who controlled the countryside while the Russians and their Afghan clients controlled the cities and highways. The rebels were supplied through the Islamic states of Iran and Pakistan, where the refugee camps doubled as training camps for the Mujaheddin.

Afghanistan
1978–84

➤ Soviet advance from 1979

⬛ main area of conflict

✦ main Soviet base

✚ Soviet airfield

⊕ airfield constructed or enlarged after 1980 by USSR

◀ refugees

— major road

The Afghan rebels learned to fight back against the helicopter gunships and were helped considerably when they were supplied with Stinger surface-to-air missiles by the Americans. Here lies a broken and twisted helicopter, successfully brought down, with all its guns and ammunition removed for further use against the Russians.

alarmed at the instability on its border, especially as it could easily mingle with that in Iran, and at the risk that an avowedly communist regime might be defeated. On 27 December 1979 it decided to take control, crudely removing the current president to replace him with someone the Soviet leaders supposed might be more popular, and sending in 85,000 Russian troops to work with Afghan forces in anti-guerrilla operations. The Afghan Army soon all but evaporated, and the Russians found themselves having to cope with the rebellion. They were unable to do much more than hold the major towns and highways. Attempts to quell the local population through direct bombardment and siege resulted in millions of refugees fleeing to Pakistan and Iran but little control. When the Americans allowed the rebels to acquire Stinger anti-air missiles the Soviet campaign found itself in further trouble.

The American response at the start of the 1980s was very much posed in Cold War terms. In the light of both the Iranian revolution and the Soviet invasion of Afghanistan, President Carter told Congress on 23 January 1980:

> Let our position be absolutely clear: an attempt by any outside force to gain control of the Persian Gulf region will be regarded as an assault on the vital interests of the United States of America, and such an assault will be repelled by any means necessary, including military force.

A Soviet tank regiment leaving for home in October 1986. The real Soviet withdrawal did not begin until Gorbachev accepted in February 1988 that Soviet forces needed to leave Afghanistan. Withdrawal was completed by February 1989, although Moscow continued to supply the regime in Kabul, which survived far longer than expected, in part because of bickering among the rebel groups.

Soviet action was interpreted as part of a drive to bring power to bear on the Gulf in an effort to secure the Soviet Union's own oil supplies and provide bases to enable it, should the need arise, to interfere with those of the West. It followed on from the apparent surge of activity by the Soviet Union and its allies in a variety of Third World conflicts during the second half of the 1970s. If Moscow expected that its investment in military power projection would pay dividends, it was soon having second thoughts. Its new friends were generally poor and isolated, and were often looking to Moscow to help quell internal dissent. Because demarcation lines in the Third World were not so clearly set, ideological loyalties fickle and military balances ambiguous, the major powers found themselves being drawn into messy regional conflicts in the mistaken belief that this was part of some grand strategic game. Specialists on the various regions warned of the limits of the East–West, bipolar model as an interpretative device, and gradually the truth of this view became apparent.

Moscow found that opportunities to exert power on a global scale were limited. Such opportunities as there were lay in the final collapse of European

During the civil war which followed Portugal's withdrawal from Angola, the Marxist MPLA gained control of most of the country, helped by Cuban forces (shown here). The main opposition came from the Western-backed UNITA. The war dragged on until a settlement in 1989, which led to the Cubans leaving Angola, but no lasting peace.

colonialism in Portuguese Africa, obligations to Vietnam as it sought to establish itself in Laos and Kampuchea and the occasional genuine defector from the West such as Ethiopia. Moreover actual applications of power were hardly satisfactory: in each case Soviet support failed to bring the desired results in Angola, Ethiopia or Kampuchea. As an investment portfolio for an aspiring imperialist the Soviet

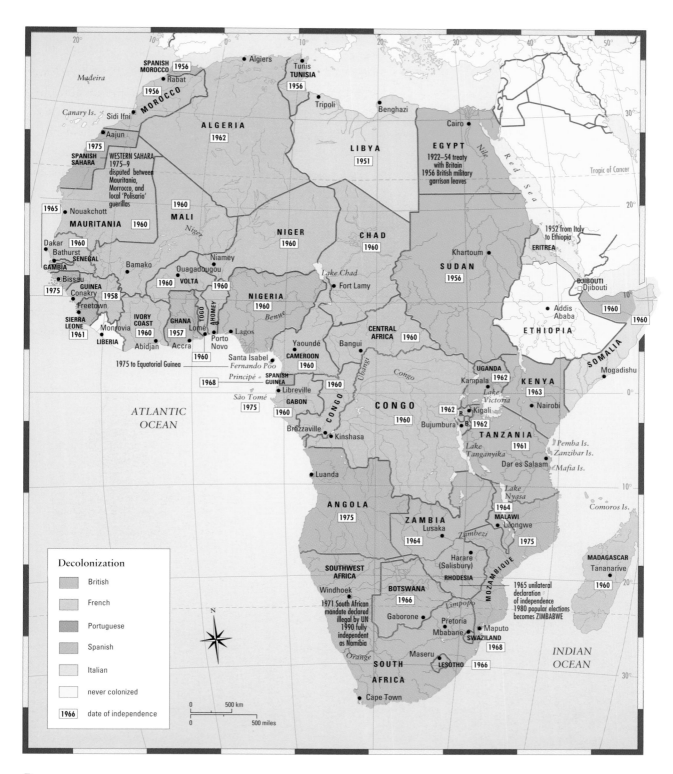

SPANISH
MOROCCO | 1956
• Algiers
Tunis •
TUNISIA | 1956

Madeira

• Rabat
1956
MOROCCO

Tripoli •
• Benghazi

Canary Is. • Sidi Ifni

Cairo •

ALGERIA
1962

LIBYA
1951

EGYPT
1922–54 treaty
with Britain
1956 British military
garrison leaves

Tropic of Cancer

• Aajun
1975

Red Sea

SPANISH
SAHARA

WESTERN SAHARA
1975–9
disputed between
Mauritania,
Morrocco, and
local 'Polisario'
guerillas

Nile

1952 from Italy
to Ethiopia
ERITREA

1965 • Nouakchott
1960

MALI
1960

NIGER
1960

CHAD
1960

Khartoum •

MAURITANIA
1960

Niger

SUDAN
1956

DJIBOUTI
Djibouti □

Dakar •
1960

Niamey •

1960

• Addis
Ababa

1960
1960

Bathurst
SENEGAL
• Bamako
Ouagadougou •
VOLTA

Lake Chad
• Fort Lamy

GAMBIA
• Bissau
GUINEA
1975
Conakry •
1958

1960
1960

NIGERIA
1960

Benue

CENTRAL
AFRICA
1960

ETHIOPIA

SOMALIA

• Mogadishu

Freetown •
IVORY
COAST
1960

GHANA
1957
TOGO
DAHOMEY
Lomé •
Porto
Novo

• Lagos

SIERRA
LEONE
1961

Monrovia •

LIBERIA

• Abidjan

Accra

1960

Yaoundé •
• Bangui

UGANDA
1962
Kampala •
1962

KENYA
1963

1960
Santa Isabel
Fernando Poo
CAMEROON
1960

Congo

• Nairobi

1975 to Equatorial Guinea

SPANISH
GUINEA

1960

• Libreville

CONGO
1960

Ubangi

*Lake
Victoria*

1962
R • Kigali

Príncipe
1968

GABON
1975
1960

• Brazzaville

CONGO
1960

1962
Bujumbura • B 1962

TANZANIA
1961

São Tomé

ATLANTIC
OCEAN

• Kinshasa

*Lake
Tanganyika*

Dar es Salaam •

Pemba Is.
Zanzibar Is.
Mafia Is.

• Luanda

0°

*Lake
Nyasa*

10°

Comoros Is.

ANGOLA
1975

1964

MALAWI
Lilongwe •
1975

ZAMBIA
1964

Lusaka •

Zambezi

MADAGASCAR
Tananarive •

1960

Harare
(Salisbury) •

RHODESIA

SOUTHWEST
AFRICA

1965 unilateral
declaration of
independence
1980 popular elections
becomes ZIMBABWE

Windhoek •

BOTSWANA
1966

MOZAMBIQUE

1971 South African
mandate declared
illegal by UN
1990 fully
independent
as Namibia

Gaborone •

Limpopo

• Maputo

Pretoria •
Mbabane •
SWAZILAND
1968

20°

Orange

Maseru •
LESOTHO
1966

INDIAN
OCEAN

SOUTH
AFRICA

30°

N

• Cape Town

Decolonization

British

French

Portuguese

Spanish

Italian

never colonized

1966 date of independence

0 ____ 500 km
0 ____ 500 miles

DECOLONIZATION

In 1960 the British prime minister Harold Macmillan warned the apartheid government of South Africa of the 'winds of change'

blowing through the African continent. Having begun the process in the 1950s, during the course of the 1960s Britain and France divested

themselves of all of their African colonies. The process was often painful – there was a vicious struggle in Algeria before it was

granted independence, while the Belgian Congo, quite unprepared for independence, soon descended into civil war.

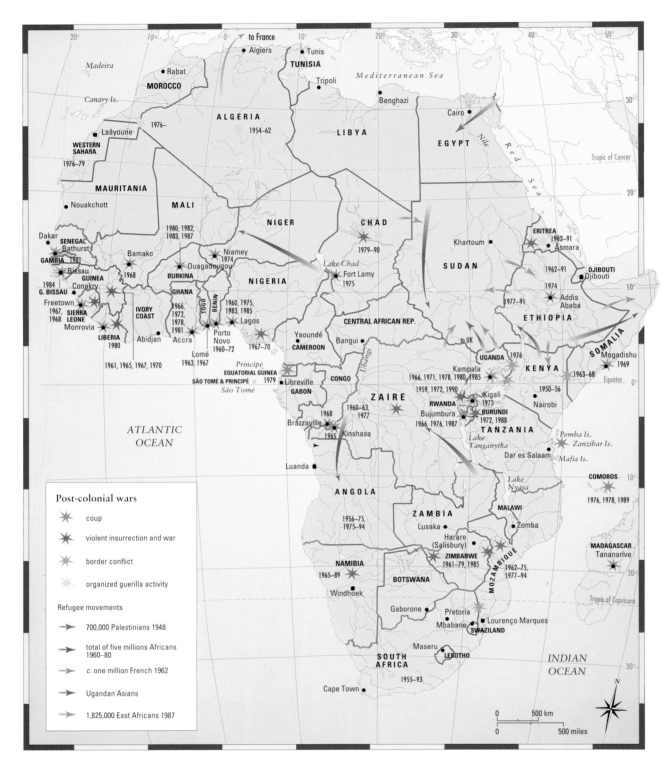

Post-colonial wars

* ✳ coup
* ✳ violent insurrection and war
* ✳ border conflict
* ✳ organized guerilla activity

Refugee movements

→ 700,000 Palestinians 1948

→ total of five millions Africans 1960–80

→ c. one million French 1962

→ Ugandan Asians

→ 1,825,000 East Africans 1987

POST-COLONIAL WARS

African countries had not been well prepared for self-government and many failed to cope with the compound problems of underdevelopment, debt, disease and despair. Most parts of the continent suffered from violent conflict, and few disputes were ever properly resolved, even after the end of the Cold War. During the 1990s Angola, Somalia, Sierra Leone and Zaire all suffered, with appalling levels of genocide in Rwanda in 1995.

Union's acquisitions appeared curiously ill-advised. The more important allies found the Soviet Union an uncongenial partner. Moreover, as NATO countries grew ever more suspicious of Soviet global ambitions and military intentions they boosted their own defence expenditures – thereby confronting Moscow with the challenge of an arms race with a technologically superior alliance.

Western involvement in these conflicts was generally confined to giving support, including weapons, to anti-Soviet factions, even though the recipients were not necessarily pro-Western. The Mujaheddin in Afghanistan, for example, tended to support all the more extreme Islamic causes, including opposition to Israel, and eventually a number took to financing their activities through drug-dealing. Although the Reagan administration was inclined to get involved in

During the mid 1970s there was vicious fighting between the Sandinista National Liberation Front and the government of Anastasio Somoza. In August 1978 the Sandinistas occupied the national palace, holding over a thousand hostages. The subsequent insurrection was initially suppressed but in summer 1979 a succession of cities fell and Somoza fled.

Central America, where a leftist group (the Sandinistas) had taken power in Nicaragua and was fighting right-wing rebels, and, next door, left-wing rebels were fighting a rightist government in El Salvador, there was no public support for intervention. After the débâcle in Beirut in 1983–4 the strictest conditions would have to be met before intervention on the ground would be considered again.

CHAPTER SEVEN

THE END OF
THE COLD WAR

EAST GERMANS flood through a breach in the Berlin Wall at Potsdamer Platz on 12 November 1989 as celebrations continue around them. The wall had been breached three days earlier.

THE END OF THE COLD WAR

T HE OVERCONFIDENT APPROACH adopted by Brezhnev during the 1970s, protecting Soviet military strength at all costs and pushing out into the Third World, had undercut liberal opinion in the West. President Carter, who had come to office warning against paranoia with regard to Soviet intentions, was forced to admit after the invasion of Afghanistan that he might have got it wrong, and that it was necessary to rebuild American military strength. For the moment, the only expression of dismay available was a boycott of the 1980 Moscow Olympics. Then came the presidency of Ronald Reagan. After the hopes of détente this was something of a shock. He showed scant interest in arms control and had a campaigning approach to the Cold War, damning the Soviet system and arguing for a major increase in military spending.

Reagan therefore reinforced the established mood shift. For a few years East–West relations were so tense that there was even talk of a 'second cold war', describing a return to the harsh days of the 1950s and 1960s that had supposedly been concluded with the onset of détente. Yet by the time Reagan came to power the Soviet leadership was becoming aware both of the strains in the system over which it was presiding and its limited ability to do much about it. Poland had been shaken by the rise to power of an independent trade union, Solidarity, led by

Solidarity leader Lech Walesa addressing workers in the Gdansk shipyard. Walesa had been an electrician at Gdansk but had lost his job for his anti-government activities. He joined a protest over food price rises at the shipyard in August 1980 and became head of the strike committee. Although the government made concessions, strikes spread and demands expanded. When independent trade unions were accepted by the government Solidarity was formed with Walesa as chairman and with massive national support. To avert a Soviet intervention the authorities declared martial law in December 1981 and Walesa was arrested.

Lech Walesa, that posed a direct challenge to communist rule, feeding on popular discontent with the mismanagement of the economy. The availability of Western technology and credits had led to the acquisition of substantial debt but not higher productivity and growth. At the end of 1981 Solidarity's power was curtailed through the imposition of martial law, with the alternative of a Soviet invasion indicated by the presence of large numbers of troops exercising close to the border. The vanguard role of the party was maintained but the economic malaise had not been addressed.

Meanwhile the gerontocratic leadership of the Communist Party of the Soviet Union was not looking very much like a vanguard. When Brezhnev died he was replaced with Yuri Andropov, a tough reformer from the KGB, but before he had a chance to make a difference he too became ill and died. He was then replaced by Konstantin Chernenko, whose emphysema was diagnosed at Andropov's funeral and who survived only a year as a stopgap. This series of ailing leaders symbolized the state of the system as a whole, which had become bureaucratized and stagnant. The planning mechanisms for heavy industry could not cope with the demands of technological innovation. The younger members of the *nomenklatura*, the ruling élite, could see the West starting to push ahead in military as much as economic strength, but were unsure whether this should be taken as a competitive challenge, in the spirit of peaceful coexistence, or the prelude to a move by the capitalist camp to crush them, perhaps even by a nuclear strike.

The new Soviet leader Konstantin Chernenko, centre, helps lay his predecessor, Yuri Andropov, to rest in 1984. Andropov had only been in power for five months after taking over from Brezhnev, and had been expected to be a modernizing leader. Chernenko was never expected to achieve much. East–West relations marked time until Reagan was re-elected and Gorbachev replaced Chernenko.

NUCLEAR OPTIONS

Why did the situation look so dangerous in the early 1980s? With Reagan US rhetoric sounded much more hawkish. Connoisseurs of strategic literature were aware of proposals for forms of nuclear victory emanating from characters who were operating on the fringes of the Reagan administration. At one point Secretary of Defense Caspar Weinberger suggested that if Reagan did not aim to prevail in war he ought to be impeached. But the problem was that at both the practical and the conceptual levels there were no compelling ideas about how to prevail in war. President Carter had bequeathed a 'countervailing' strategy designed to convince the Soviet Union that there were no circumstances in which it could prevail, and that was about as far as the problem could be taken. Few were comfortable about talking about mutual assured destruction, although that remained a reasonable description. Mutual assured countervailing was less catchy but perhaps a better description of the strategic interaction.

A nuclear victory would require a first strike, but as there could be no guarantee of eliminating the enemy's retaliatory capability it was hard to see why any leader would take the risk. One proposal was to aim for the enemy's political and military command-and-control centres in so-called *decapitation* attacks, in the hope that leaderless forces would not launch their weapons. Could this be guaranteed, and without leaders with whom would it be possible to negotiate an end to the war? Another problem was the trade-off between preparing systems suitable for mounting an offensive and ensuring invulnerability to an enemy offensive. The Americans developed a large ICBM – known as M-X for 'Missile Experimental' – but could not work out how to protect it from a surprise attack. Numerous proposals were considered, including launching the missile from aircraft, or moving it along underground trenches or around a racetrack, and with a choice of many shelters to confuse Soviet targeting. None met the necessary environmental, financial or practical criteria. For a brief moment the Reagan administration tried to sell the concept of 'dense pack'. This involved putting missiles so close together that the electromagnetic pulse released by the first explosions of the attacking warheads would have the fratricidal effect of disabling the warheads of the following missiles. Eventually it was decided to deploy a number of M-X missiles in existing fixed silos and to stop worrying so much about the scenario that placed such great store by their vulnerability.

Given that most major war scenarios arose out of conflict in Europe, an alternative approach to prevailing might be to limit nuclear exchanges to Europe. During the Carter years a controversy arose around the enhanced radiation reduced-blast weapon, better known as the neutron bomb. This was a weapon for use on a battlefield, rather than against cities. It was designed with reduced heat and blast effects, relying on extra radiation to disable tank crews. The furore that soon surrounded this weapon, inaccurately described as a capitalist bomb, which killed people while leaving buildings intact, and the reluctance of his NATO allies to ask for its deployment, led Carter to shelve the project in 1978. The outcry generated by the neutron bomb, especially in western Europe, meant that the next major nuclear programme was greeted with even greater suspicion by protest groups, who feared the consequences of a new round in the arms race and suspected that it was an instrument of a limited nuclear philosophy.

There was evidence of a Soviet limited nuclear war philosophy, and even some deployments to match in the 1970s: a new medium-range aircraft (Backfire) and, most controversially, a new intermediate-range missile (SS-20). The idea appeared to be that the conventional phase of a war in Europe could be used to prepare the ground, for example by conventional moves against NATO nuclear assets, for a decisive but geographically confined nuclear strike. Critically, it was assumed that if the continental United States was left unscathed, Washington would not order retaliation against the Soviet homeland, even though other members of the Warsaw Pact might suffer grievously. The strategy depended on an implicit deal to establish the territories of both superpowers as sanctuaries. Carter's countervailing strategy was in fact designed to deny Moscow confidence that, at any point in escalating from crisis to all-out nuclear war, it could expect to so dominate the fighting that it would force NATO to surrender. It was in line with this strategy, in December 1979, that NATO agreed to introduce new intermediate-range missiles of its own: 464 Tomahawk cruise missiles and 108 Pershing-2 ballistic missiles. These would be deployed from late 1983 onwards to deal with these various problems. Britain, Germany, Italy, Belgium and the Netherlands (the last two only tentatively) agreed to host these new

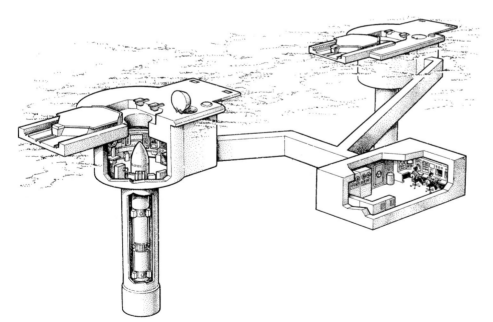

MISSILE SILO

The sliding door of a missile silo is designed to withstand blast effects and the frame within which the missile is held to absorb shock from nearby nuclear explosions. The silo has to allow enough space to accommodate the hot gases emitted during launch. An underground control post would be responsible for a number of missiles (ten in the case of US Minuteman ICBMs).

missiles. It was also agreed to enter into negotiations with the Soviet Union on the possibility of reducing the actual and planned numbers of the missiles of both sides. This became known as the 'dual-track' decision. Although these missiles came to be twinned in public debate and in arms control negotiations, their roles were different. The key feature of the NATO missiles was that they could hit Soviet territory. By being based in Europe they could be taken to be underlining the point that a major conventional war could lead to nuclear strikes against the Soviet homeland. Therefore rather than serving as instruments of limited nuclear war, as the protest movements claimed, they undermined any possibility that a nuclear war could be limited.

None the less the NATO decision triggered a surge of anti-nuclear sentiment throughout Europe. Although the anti-nuclear movement offered elaborate analyses of the reckless turn in US strategy, much of its support came more from a basic repugnance towards the idea that Western governments could even begin to contemplate circumstances in which they would unleash a nuclear terror. In the United States the 'freeze' movement played on the same fears, arguing for no new nuclear deployments. Western governments might be confident of popular

The Tomahawk cruise missile in its nuclear-tipped ground-launched version was originally deployed in NATO countries during the early 1980s, sparking off major anti-nuclear protests. Later the submarine-launched version, as shown below, with conventional warheads, became a regular feature of American military operations, used in the Gulf and the Balkans during the 1990s.

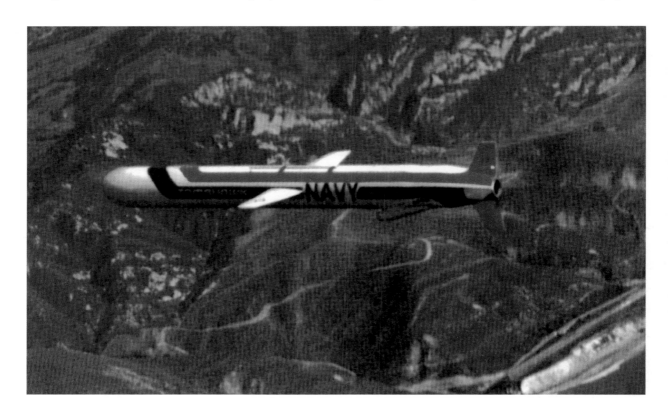

majorities for maintaining nuclear weapons as a form of insurance but there was clearly deep unease at any suggestion of actual preparations for nuclear war. Civil defence provisions such as fallout shelters and evacuation procedures, rather than being seen as prudent precautions against a worst case scenario, were seen as somehow reckless and sinister because they denied the civilization-crushing reality of a nuclear war. Scientific analysis suggesting that massive nuclear exchanges could have catastrophic climatic results – a 'nuclear winter' – supported the view that the survivors would envy the dead. There were real political constraints on the ability of Western governments to pursue anything but the most restrained nuclear strategy.

The intense debates of the early 1980s brought to the fore a series of problems with nuclear deterrence which had long been appreciated by strategists and policy-makers but had been considered too difficult – and in practical terms too irrelevant – to warrant public ventilation. The protest movements left in their wake a general dissatisfaction with flexible response. Governments found themselves addressing the issue of 'what do we do if deterrence fails' as a real strategic problem rather than a remote hypothesis. Now also, instead of the old issue of whether Western Europe could rely on the United States to put itself at nuclear risk in order to deter a conventional invasion by the Warsaw Pact, the popular concern was whether Western Europe might be put at nuclear risk by the United States in its pursuit of a global confrontation with the Soviet Union.

President Reagan's announcement in March 1983 that he intended to spend

The RAF base at Greenham Common near Newbury, where 160 American cruise missiles came to be based, became the focal point for the British anti-nuclear movement. Here demonstrators link hands around the perimeter fence.

billions of dollars exploring the possibility of strategic defences capable of blocking missile attacks directed against the United States and its allies reflected similar sentiments to those of the protestors. Would not protection against nuclear attack, asked Reagan, be better than vengeance? Should not every effort

American President Ronald Reagan and Prime Minister Margaret Thatcher symbolized the Conservative ascendancy of the 1980s in their rigorous free market economic policies and robust anti-communism. This ideological affinity hid substantial policy differences. This meeting in December 1984 involved an effort by Thatcher to persuade Reagan not to get so carried away with the rhetoric surrounding his Strategic Defence Initiative as to undermine the credibility of nuclear deterrence.

be made to render ballistic missiles 'impotent and obsolete'? The reason that this question was not taken at face value, and as Reagan intended, was that the answer offered was problematic, and it was not hard to imagine a more disturbing purpose. Reagan's vision, involving space-based lasers and multiple forms of interception, was always far-fetched. After many decades and great expense there would still be doubts over whether an effective defence would be manageable, given the low margin of error. Even if ballistic missiles were blocked, bombers and cruise missiles would remain. If, however, the aim was only to develop ballistic missile defence as a backstop to a first-strike capability, a means of coping with the much-reduced Soviet threat that might survive a surprise attack, then it started to look more credible. If it were possible for a defensive shield to parry the Soviet nuclear sword, then the American sword would enjoy an unparalleled freedom of manoeuvre.

The announcement of the Strategic Defense Initiative added to a tense 1983. The year ended with the Soviet Union walking out of the Geneva arms control talks as cruise missiles were introduced into Britain and Germany, and an enormous row over the shooting down of a Korean airliner by Soviet air defences. We now know that the KGB had all but convinced itself that NATO was about to launch a pre-emptive strike. A NATO exercise of November 1983, ABEL-ARCHER-83, simulated raising the alert level of US nuclear forces and was at one point to have involved all top American policy-makers. This started to appear in

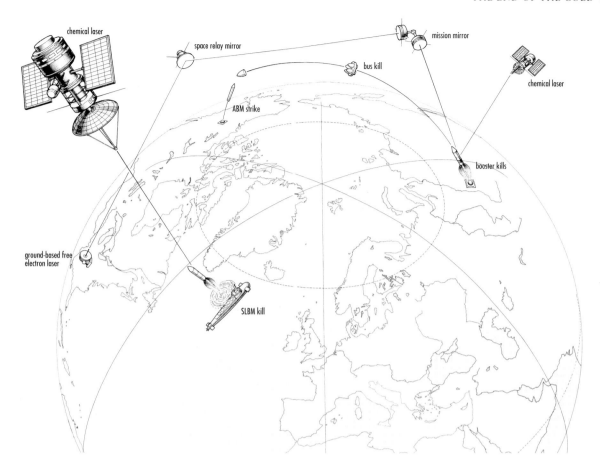

chemical laser
space relay mirror
mission mirror
bus kill
ABM strike
chemical laser
booster kills
ground-based free
electron laser
SLBM kill

Moscow as a possible cover for the real thing. The Russians raised the alert level of their forces. Washington realized that matters might be getting out of hand and began to send more reassuring signals.

At the start of 1985, with Reagan re-elected, the view from Moscow changed dramatically. A new, relatively young leader, Mikhail Gorbachev, took over, determined to modernize his country and escape from the dead hand of the arms race. Moreover, Reagan's doubts about the morality and durability of deterrence were genuine. As his favoured method of escape, the Strategic Defense Initiative, was unworkable he found himself arguing instead for radical disarmament. This all came together in a remarkable summit at Reykjavik in November 1986 when Reagan and Gorbachev engaged in competitive bidding to demonstrate just how far they were prepared to go to eliminate the various categories of nuclear weapons. At Reykjavik the sticking point was still the Strategic Defense Initiative but within months Gorbachev had realized that his demands that it be scrapped were providing an argument for those who believed it might just work ('if it is so useless why is Gorbachev so hostile?'). By December 1987 it was possible to agree to remove all Pershings and ground-launched cruise missiles in return for all SS-20s. For a while there was a debate in NATO about whether or not some short-range weapons were needed but this soon became overtaken by events. There was no reason to have nuclear weapons in West Germany that could only hit East Germany once the two were planning unification.

STAR WARS

President Reagan's Strategic Defense Initiative involved a variety of different forms of interception. The most challenging type would be at the boost phase of a missile, before it could unleash its package of warheads and decoys. This would require excellent intelligence and an ability to turn immense power on to the newly launched missile almost immediately. A variety of forms of directed energy weapons were explored but the technological demands were extreme, and in some cases appeared to challenge the laws of physics. There could have been little confidence in the reliability of any deployed system.

THE BERLIN WALL FALLS

There is an argument that the arms race, and perhaps more particularly the Strategic Defense Initiative, triggered the end of the Cold War. It was certainly the case that Gorbachev found the proportion of GDP devoted to defence extraordinarily high and realized that his country was finding it difficult to compete in all areas of advanced weapons technology. His military were among the most ardent reformers because they could see that unless the economy was modernized there was no hope for the modernization of the armed forces. But it was the underlying rottenness and inefficiency of the Soviet system that had created this predicament, and by the time Gorbachev came to power, things were too far gone for him to be able to make much difference.

Détente had provided an excuse for Moscow to avoid confronting its fundamental weaknesses. No serious restrictions were put on its defence spending: Moscow continued to believe that it could use its military strength to face down its communist rivals in China and to gain footholds in the Third World. It used deals with the West to address – unsuccessfully – deficiencies in its technology, grain production and finances. It did nothing to remedy the sense of cynicism and illegitimacy surrounding the claims of the Communist Party or rein in the repressive apparatus that sustained its 'vanguard' role.

By the time of martial law in Poland in 1981 NATO planners had few war contingencies other than a crisis resulting from an urge to independence within the Warsaw Pact. Such a crisis was not anticipated eagerly as a moment of hope but feared as one of extreme danger. It had been drummed into the Western security community that nuclear deterrence worked because it dissuaded both sides from launching military adventures against the other out of a fear of a terrible retribution. The conventions of the superpower relationship had it that neither could interfere directly in each other's 'sphere of influence'. But all this meant was that a mutual recognition of the dangers inherent in any attempt to resolve the underlying ideological antagonism through a contest of arms turned it into an attritional contest of social systems.

It was on this basis that scenarios for a NATO–Warsaw Pact confrontation were identified, built on the possibility that the *nomenklatura* would not give up its privileged position, nor the Soviet Union its East European buffer, without a fight. The intervention in Afghanistan in the last days of the 1970s warned that the Kremlin might attempt to crush any opposition with force but also – and

possibly more dangerously – that it might fail, with the risk of a conflict spilling over into the surrounding region. In the early 1980s in particular, those acknowledging the internal contradictions within the Soviet system did not allow for the speed and comparatively graceful nature of communism's eventual demise. The economic system was poor but the military position was still strong. The Russian people had been obliged to make sacrifices and suffer terribly in the past to ensure the survival of the communist system. Who was to say that they would not do so again in the future? Until well into the 1980s an odd debate was conducted in NATO about whether the greatest danger came from mean and hungry Russians, who might take reckless action out of desperation, or fat and contented Russians, who might have less cause for desperate action but the wherewithal to conclude it successfully.

Because NATO seemed much more argumentative than the Warsaw Pact it was assumed that its natural coherence was less. Even the absence of a strong sense of imminent threat could be a security challenge in itself, perhaps providing

The novelty of a relatively young Soviet leader, comfortable with ordinary people, offering reformist ideas and bold arms control initiatives, captured the West's imagination. 'Gorbymania' was especially evident among Germans, who hoped to see an end to the Cold War that had left it on the front line for over four decades. In the Soviet Union, where the negative effects of his policies seemed more pronounced, he was somewhat less popular.

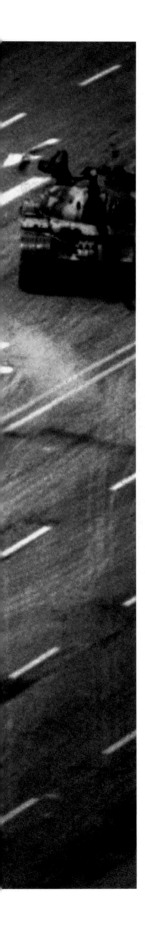

the United States with an excuse to opt out of its European commitments or Germany with enticements away from its Western anchor by promises of unification. Such concerns underestimated NATO's foundation of shared values and the fact that at times of relative tranquillity there was no obvious need to experiment with security arrangements one way or the other.

Gorbachev was appalled at the gap between the party rhetoric proclaiming constant progress and achievement and the dismal reality of corruption, shortages and shoddy goods, and introduced into the political lexicon the slogans *perestroika* (restructuring) and *glasnost* (openness). As he was uncomfortable with the idea that communist power must rest on the threat of brute force, and wanted the military burden on the Soviet economy reduced, he sought a new and more deep-rooted détente with the West. He believed none the less that the Communist Party could still be an agency of radical change, by turning on those who had developed their privileges and sought protection from incompetence in the party's name. It also required a similar confrontation in eastern Europe, despite the fact that there hardliners were generally still in charge so that the alternative was not a reformist party but no party at all.

Only belatedly did Gorbachev fully appreciate the link between Soviet military power and the maintenance of a Soviet sphere of influence. The Soviet military had suffered through its failure to defeat the Mujaheddin in Afghanistan. Yet Gorbachev was still required to rule out explicitly the use of force to sustain the Soviet position in eastern Europe for the change to follow its comfortingly graceful course. The events that followed the sudden removal of the repressive constraint imposed by Soviet military power in early 1989 are a testimony of sorts to its importance up to this time. If Gorbachev had insisted on following the practice of his predecessors in this regard, there is no evidence that the West would have done much about it. In the summer of 1989, when faced with peaceful demonstrations by the young, urban élite in favour of democratic change the Chinese decided to crush this challenge. So it was within eastern Europe that the crucial moments came as military units had to decide whether or not they should fire on their own people. The

While communist parties were giving up in Europe, events in China showed what could happen when a party decided to cling to power. On the night of 3/4 June 1989, after weeks during which Tiananmen Square, in the centre of Beijing, had been occupied by thousands of students and others hoping for a more open society, the troops were sent in to clear the square. This famous picture captures a moment of defiance as a single student stands in front of a column of tanks.

role of force as the ultimate arbiter of power was largely confirmed by its absence, although on occasion by its presence, as in Romania in December 1989 and then in a series of internal power struggles in Russia.

Romania, led by the autocratic Nicolae Ceausescu, had once been courted by the West because of its independence from Moscow. The real sources of subversion in the Soviet system were not wayward dictators but communist states that were starting to develop pluralist systems. During 1989 Solidarity moved into government in Poland, while the Hungarian Communist Party encouraged

One communist dictator who refused to go quietly was Nicolae Ceausescu. Even after he had been summarily tried and shot after trying to flee Bucharest, the Romanian capital was the scene of heavy fighting, pitting the army and civilians against the Securitate secret police.

greater democracy and the development of freer markets. It was when Hungary opened its border with Austria that the real changes began, as East Germans began to take their vacations in Hungary with no intention of returning home. These opportunities to leave, coupled with regular demonstrations centred on Leipzig against the regime, came to a crunch in November 1989. Gorbachev had made it clear to Erich Honecker, the hard line party boss in East Germany, that he could expect no support if he tried to crack down on the demonstrators. The Berlin Wall suddenly appeared beside the point. Legitimacy was draining away daily from the regime. When demonstrators decided one day just to walk through the checkpoint nobody felt able to stop them, and soon the wall was being dismantled as part of a great popular celebration.

The next month, with communism in full retreat throughout Europe, Gorbachev met US President Bush in Malta for a pre-arranged summit. Gorbachev's spokesman, Gennady Gerasimov, quipped that the Cold War had lasted from Yalta (the 'Big Three' meeting in early 1945 which had first addressed the problems of the post-war world) to Malta. The risk of a great military confrontation had all but evaporated, but it took until the end of 1991 before the dynamic of change had run its course.

The first and potentially the most serious change was the unification of Germany. Memories of two world wars had left a lingering fear of an over-strong Germany as much amongst its western as its eastern neighbours. It seemed much safer divided; as one French politician put it, 'I love Germany so much I want two of them'. Prime Minister Thatcher of Britain made her anxieties explicit. President Mitterrand of France was also anxious but he decided that the best option was to tie Germany further into the institutions of Europe and Chancellor Kohl was happy to oblige. A European Germany was offered rather than a German Europe. In practice the demands of unification weakened German economic strength.

Back in Moscow, Gorbachev's problem was that his party was the only unifying force in the Soviet Union, but it was now discredited. There was seething discontent in many republics, resulting in massive demonstrations and vicious intercommunal conflicts, particularly in the Baltic and the Caucasus. In August 1991 a group of old, and not very competent, Politburo hands decided to depose Gorbachev on the grounds that he was about to approve legislation that would have undermined the state. The Union of Soviet Socialist Republics was soon unlikely to be any of those things, other than possibly republics. Boris Yeltsin, who had already broken with Gorbachev for not being radical enough and was leading the Russian Federation, stepped in to defy the plotters, who had not secured the full backing of the army and security services and soon lost their nerve. Gorbachev was undone not by the plotters but by his apparent willingness, as he returned from his brief captivity, to contemplate a continuing role for the Communist Party. By the end of 1991 the Soviet Union had split into fifteen separate states.

When a group of diehards in Moscow made a half-hearted attempt at a coup and put Gorbachev under house arrest, it was Boris Yeltsin who served as the rallying point for Russians who refused to accept the coup. The coup did effectively leave Gorbachev powerless, but his loss was to Yeltsin rather than the old communists.

CHAPTER EIGHT

THE WAR THAT DID NOT HAPPEN

IRAQIS WITH EVERY AVAILABLE VEHICLE full of plunder from Kuwait tried to escape from advancing American troops during the 1991 Gulf War. North of Kuwait City they were caught by allied aircraft. Pilots spoke of a 'turkey shoot' and the immediate impression was of mass carnage, sufficient to encourage President Bush to bring the war to an end, but in fact most Iraqis had fled as soon as the bombing started.

THE WAR THAT DID NOT HAPPEN

For those optimistic that the end of the Cold War would bring peace to Europe, the succession of wars surrounding the collapse of Yugoslavia – in Croatia, Bosnia and then Kosovo, with Macedonia continually on the brink – was profoundly depressing. In Bosnia the major European powers intervened under the auspices of the UN, first to deliver food and medical supplies, and then to take on the Serbs, who were believed to be largely responsible for the sharpening of ethnic conflicts in the area.

MOST WARS THAT HAPPEN catch at least one of the belligerents by surprise and sometimes both. Neither NATO nor the Warsaw Pact wished – or intended – to fight a third world war, but accepted that they were caught in a terrible paradox. They would have to fight only if they gave the appearance of being unready for a fight. So almost up to the last days of the Cold War the preparations were serious, expensive and intensive. Analyses were undertaken concerning such matters as the mobilization potential of the two alliances, how this might affect the balance of forces during the first days of a conflict, and what difference it would make if NATO tried to cope with the onslaught through a static or a mobile defence or resorted to short-range nuclear forces. By this time there were no expectations of imminent conflict. Few actually believed that their computer printouts would ever spring to life on a battlefield. The analyses of weapons and doctrines and balances took the shape they did because there was no other serious starting point for the purposes of force-planning and arms control.

It had become hard to think through the circumstances that would trigger a war in the first place. So potent were the nightmarish images of a third world war that there really was no good reason why any moderately sane leader would start one deliberately. So difficult did it become to generate credible scenarios for the

outbreak of war that eventually nobody bothered to try. It had become even harder to work out how such a war would end. A universal consensus postulated utter death and destruction as the likely conclusion. If that was inevitable, what was the requirement for conventional military forces? The generals were not asked to devise plans for a decisive battlefield victory. Their task was largely to reinforce deterrence by creating conditions which might bring about an Armageddon, engulfing them along with everyone else. The best that could be offered was an opportunity to hold a defensive line to allow sufficient time for second thoughts and active negotiations, and so interrupt the powder trail before it reached its explosive climax. Because the main deterrent was nuclear rather than conventional, it had always been an uphill task to convince governments to provide the resources to mount a serious defence. Because the most likely source of chronic instability was judged to be a breakdown in alliance, the role of the armed forces became increasingly one of reinforcing the alliance by demonstrating commitments to mutual security, burden-sharing, and a fair spread of rights and responsibilities.

Once the Cold War could be consigned to history the budget cuts began in earnest. The average Western country cut its armed forces by around a quarter. Finance ministers, always the greatest enthusiasts for disarmament, continued to press for more reductions, and it took about a decade after the end of the Cold War before defence budgets stabilized and even started to creep up again. The issue was whether there was any threat that justified a serious effort. After 1989

Bosnian Muslims were often rounded up by the Serbs and kept in camps. The fate of these prisoners caused outrage when they were discovered. They were somewhat luckier than those rounded up in Srebrenica in July 1995, thousands of whom were killed.

there were those in NATO who feared that Moscow might revert to its bad old ways and wished to keep up the insurance policy, but once the Warsaw Pact and then the Soviet Union ceased to exist this lost credibility.

Of course from Moscow's perspective matters looked quite different. As former allies clamoured, some successfully, to join NATO, and as NATO found an activist role for itself in the Balkans, the position could appear quite parlous. The Russians' demeanour was not helped by the inner collapse of what had once been a formidable fighting force. Conscripts failed to turn up for duty, officers were not paid and lost their privileges, equipment was neither maintained nor replaced, morale collapsed. When they had to deal with a local uprising in the province of Chechnya, they failed. Not surprisingly, the conclusion of this was that they found themselves dependent upon their nuclear arsenal to deter NATO from any aggression against Russia, although exactly what Western countries might covet within Russian territory was difficult to imagine.

For their part NATO countries could get irritated with Russia when it acted as a diplomatic spoiler to protect old friends, such as Iraq or Yugoslavia. They largely worried about its weakness more than its strength, about the environmental consequences of its deteriorating nuclear submarine force, which it could not afford to decommission properly, or the dangers of mismanaged nuclear forces, or the impact of social and economic collapse. There were some who believed that its place as the main challenger of the United States would be bound to be taken by Germany or Japan, although neither showed any inclination to do so, or by China. China certainly expected to be treated with respect, with a huge population and a growing economy, but its ambitions were largely regional. The strategic issues in Asia were largely those left over from the early years of the Cold War: how the divided China and Korea might eventually be unified, and the dangers if one side resisted the process.

One of Iraq's main responses to the overwhelming conventional military strength of the Allies was to use old Scud missiles, fired at the limits of their range, and with only conventional warheads, at Saudi Arabia and Israel. Here a Scud missile that has landed in downtown Riyadh, possibly helped down by a Patriot missile, is under examination.

THE GULF WAR

Two other, medium-sized powers kept NATO's military busy in the years after the end of the Cold War. The most remarkable episode was the 1991 Gulf War. In August 1990 Iraq seized Kuwait, largely for economic reasons, although there was also a long-standing territorial claim. This was a blatant act of aggression involving two of the most important oil-producing countries. President Bush and

Prime Minister Thatcher decided immediately that Saddam Hussein must be stopped before he tried to take Saudi Arabia as well. The international community was prepared to put economic pressure on Iraq but reluctant to contemplate military action until it became apparent that Saddam was not prepared to budge and was slowly dismantling Kuwaiti society and economy, by physically transporting the bulk of Kuwait's assets back to Iraq. In addition, there were concerns not only that he was seeking to develop an arsenal of mass destruction but that he would also use chemical weapons (as he already had done against Iranians and Kurds) and maybe even nuclear weapons.

On 16 January 1991 an air war began against Iraq which eventually created the conditions for a land offensive in February that had Iraqi forces scampering out of Kuwait as fast they could. In the end the war turned out to be remarkably

DESERT STORM

The Iraqis had been expecting that coalition forces would attempt to retake Kuwait by means of either an amphibious landing or a direct thrust across the Saudi border to Kuwait City, and had not appreciated the capacity of the coalition to move its forces undetected so that they could sweep through Iraqi territory in an effort to envelop Iraqi forces before they could escape. The Iraqis retreated quickly and so the coalition's 'left hook' could not quite close off the escape route in time.

easy, although it had been advertised in advance as a rather difficult enterprise, taking on an extremely large army that was geared to inflicting massive casualties on Western forces, which Saddam believed would deter the coalition forces from prolonged combat. In this he wholly underestimated the degree of outrage in the West at his behaviour and also the substantial improvements in American capabilities, with the introduction of 'smart' weapons and coherent doctrine, both drawing on advanced information technologies.

The Allies fought the war against Iraq on the basis of concepts and equipment originally developed for a war against the Warsaw Pact in central Europe. If there had still been any prospect of a NATO–Warsaw Pact confrontation, then the results of the Gulf War would have been encouraging. The staff college exercises, the tactical ploys and the training appeared to have proved themselves. Advanced weapons performed as the manufacturers' brochures said they would. Perhaps the difference was that when the military confrontation came, Iraq failed to put up a serious fight. Its small navy had no place to hide and was virtually eliminated. The air force essentially gave up

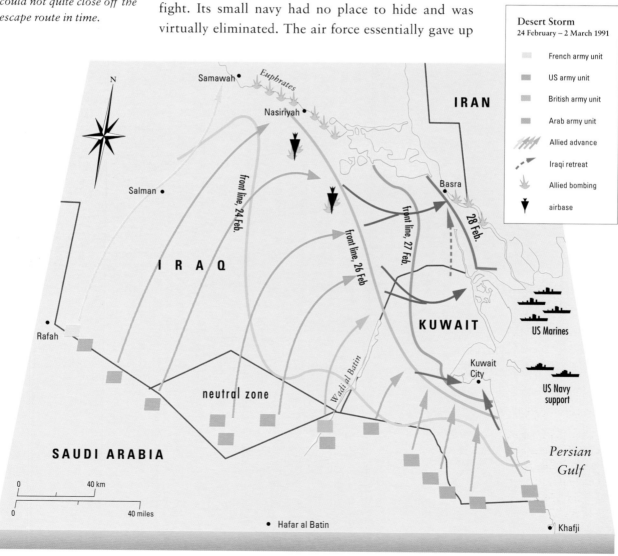

and ran for cover to Iran. As a result the Iraqi capacity to sustain a war for any length of time was unpicked, while its land forces had no effective air cover against an enemy about equal in numbers but extraordinarily well endowed in equipment and with secure supply lines.

Despite the advanced publicity which spoke of it as capable of doing enormous damage to the West, the much-vaunted Iraqi Army crumbled within days. It was judged to be half a million strong inside Kuwait and on the Kuwaiti border, experienced in protracted defence, well dug in and supported by numerous artillery and tanks. It turned out that in most respects Iraqi strength had been overestimated. It had been flattered by successes in a very different sort of conflict with Iran and then inflated through a focus on its quantities of manpower, tanks, aircraft and so on rather than an investigation into its quality. Though some units put up token resistance, for many soldiers it was clear that their basic tactical consideration for some time had been how best to surrender.

The Gulf War led to the proclamation of a revolution in military affairs in the United States, as precision weaponry combined with information technology to allow for forms of warfare that did

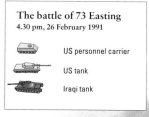

The battle of 73 Easting
4.30 pm, 26 February 1991

US personnel carrier

US tank

Iraqi tank

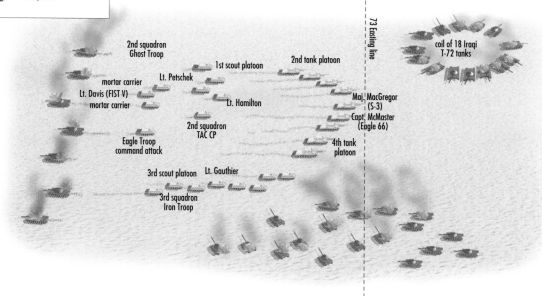

THE BATTLE OF 73 EASTING

One of the toughest battles of the Gulf War was at 73 Easting, a point on the longitudinal line on the US Army map. Three troops from an American cavalry regiment, in Bradley fighting vehicles with M-1 tanks, were surprised to find themselves tangling with the relatively unscathed Tawakalna Division of the Republican Guard with T-72 tanks, backed by artillery. The Americans got through using the superior firepower of their tank guns and anti-tank weapons. It provided a significant demonstration of the qualitative superiority of American forces.

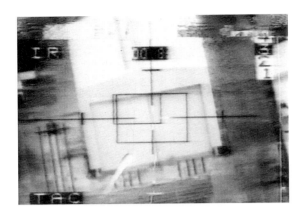

The Gulf War demonstrated the advances in precision guidance achieved over the previous two decades. Weapons were shown hitting targets accurately, with the minimum of damage to surrounding civilian life, even to the front doors of a bunker.

Iraqi soldiers did not fight for long in the Gulf. Here a line of prisoners is led away through the desert, past vehicles of the US Marines 2nd Division.

not depend on brute force but rather involved the efficient application of power to the most vulnerable parts of the enemy's military machine. The line of technological development was real enough, and it caught out Iraqi strategy because that strategy depended upon opportunities to kill large numbers of Western forces. Noting Vietnam and Lebanon, Saddam Hussein had assumed that fear of casualties was the West's greatest vulnerability. 'Yours is not a country that can lose ten thousand men in a single day', he told American Ambassador April Glaspie just before he took Kuwait. But the only conclusion to be drawn from the Gulf War was that there was an unbridgeable gap between advanced military powers and those merely aspiring to this status so long as a war was fought on a wholly conventional basis. This gap had been hidden because engagements between advanced military powers and Third World countries would often take the form of guerrilla warfare. Superpowers could be humbled, as were the Americans in Vietnam or the Russians in Afghanistan, by an irregular enemy refusing to engage regular forces on their own terms.

After the Gulf War, as the opponents of the West internalized this message, it could be assumed that they would do their utmost to avoid regular warfare. They would either threaten the civil societies of the West by using weapons of mass destruction or terrorism or, equally likely, would seek to bog them down in prolonged irregular campaigns, imposing unacceptable casualties until Western public opinion argued for retreat. The wars resulting from the break-up of

Yugoslavia during the 1990s saw the West reluctant to intervene directly and, when it did so, preferring the application of air power to land power. But air power had inherent limitations, even though its accuracy was remarkable. The revolution in military affairs turned out to be of limited relevance. It described a future Great Power war, which, at least for the time being, was the most unlikely of scenarios.

The Cold War represented the culmination of the Great Power politics of the nineteenth and twentieth centuries. It followed the basic themes of balance of power and competitions for influence, producing a stark polarization between two competing social systems. The potential consequences of making the choice through war were so terrible, not least because of the likelihood of nuclear exchanges, that in the end a stable balance of power was accomplished. This military stalemate allowed the choice between competing social systems to be made by reference to their performance in times of peace. We can only guess at who might have won a NATO–Warsaw Pact clash; we know that communism lost the ideological war.

Even after the Gulf War ended, oil wells fired by the Iraqis burned uncontrollably, spewing out a toxic fog which hovered over the area for some six months before all the fires could be put out. In the foreground is a destroyed Iraqi tank.

OVERLEAF: *The departure of Soviet forces did not end the fighting in Afghanistan. A woman mourns for her brother killed in a rocket attack.*

BIOGRAPHIES

AMERICANS

HARRY TRUMAN (1884–1972)

A last minute choice as Roosevelt's vice-president in 1944, he soon became president after FDR's death in April 1945. He was thrown into the international conferences concerning the shape of the post-war world. He proved to be decisive and tough, gaining a shock re-election in 1948. He set out American Cold War policy with the doctrine of containment, established the CIA and the National Security Council and authorized the development of the hydrogen bomb. In 1950 he led his country into the Korean War.

DWIGHT D. EISENHOWER (1890–1969)

Hailed as the architect of the Allied victory in Europe in 1945, he was recalled from civilian life in 1951 by Truman to become the first Supreme Allied Commander, Europe (SACEUR). In June 1952 he decided to run for president and won as the Republican nominee. He soon extricated the USA from Korea. He did little to contain McCarthyism. During his second term his health was poor and he appeared passive in the face of a more dynamic communist threat, especially after being caught out by the Soviet Sputnik in October 1957 and the U-2 crisis of May 1960. None the less he remained extremely popular, managing to combine a strong anti-communism with a refusal to be panicked into an arms race.

JOHN KENNEDY (1917–63)

Went into politics after an active war and short stint as a journalist and won the 1960 presidential election. Initially undermined by the Bay of Pigs fiasco in April 1961, he recovered his poise, taking firm stands on Berlin and then on Soviet missiles in Cuba, while always looking for an opportunity to negotiate. In 1963 he signed and obtained the ratification of the partial test ban treaty. In November 1963 he was assassinated by Lee Harvey Oswald. Whether Oswald was acting alone or as part of a conspiracy has been a source of endless fascination ever since.

LYNDON JOHNSON (1908–73)

Suddenly became president after the assassination of John Kennedy in November 1963. His determination to press forward on civil rights and social reform was responsible for a landslide presidential victory in 1964, against a hawkish Republican, Barry Goldwater. His ambitious domestic agenda was overtaken by his commitment to the Vietnam War. There was a lack of clarity in military and political objectives, and as the burden of the war grew it became progressively unpopular. In March 1968 he combined a bid to de-escalate the war and start negotiations with an announcement that he would not be standing for another term.

RICHARD NIXON (1913–94)

Enjoyed a meteoric political rise as a dogged anti-communist, and as Eisenhower's vice-president. Narrowly defeated by Kennedy in the 1960 election, he bounced back in 1968 and won a narrow victory himself over Hubert Humphrey. He limited Vietnam's political impact through ending the draft and relying more on American air power and Vietnamese ground forces. Widening the war in 1970 to include communist sanctuaries in Cambodia led to an upsurge in anti-war protest. This prompted activities against the protesters, culminating in the break-in at the Democratic Party headquarters in Watergate in 1972. This scandal would have led to Nixon's impeachment had he not resigned in 1974. There were positive and, given his background, surprising achievements during Nixon's period in office, notably improved relations with both China and Russia.

JIMMY CARTER (1924–)

Began his career in the US Navy working on submarines, entered politics in 1962 and was elected governor of Georgia in 1970, where he ended segregation. The surprising Democratic Party candidate for president in 1976, he won against Gerald Ford, who had only taken over from Nixon in 1974 because of Watergate. His keen promotion of human rights as president was in tension with his desire to improve relations with the Soviet Union. Eventually he agreed a new strategic arms treaty with Moscow, in spite of domestic hostility aroused by from the Soviet military build-up, but Senate ratification had to be suspended because of Afghanistan. His presidency was doomed by his inability to deal with the Iranian hostage crisis. After leaving office he became a travelling statesman, mediating on conflicts involving Nicaragua, North Korea and Haiti.

Ronald Reagan (1911–)

Followed a Hollywood career to become Republican governor of California from 1966 to 1974. He defeated Carter for the presidency in 1980. After surviving an assassination attempt, he embarked on higher defence spending and reduced taxes. To reduce dependence on nuclear deterrence he launched his Strategic Defense Initiative in 1983. More successful was his pursuit of arms control with Gorbachev which led in 1987 to the treaty eliminating intermediate-range nuclear forces. His tendency to leave policy-making to his aides was responsible for the confusion of the Iran–Contra scandal of 1986.

Russians

Joseph Stalin (1879–1953)

Became secretary general of the Communist Party's Central Committee in 1922 and used this position to see off every possible rival, enforce farm collectivization and rapid industrialization. With purges and show trials he ensured his primacy. Shocked by early reverses in the Second World War, his patience and ruthlessness allowed him to lead his country to victory. He imposed his will on Eastern Europe while taking a belligerent stance toward his war-time allies, Britain and the United States. The terror continued at home, concluded only by his sudden death in 1953.

Nikita Khrushchev (1894–1971)

Was an old Bolshevik, working with Stalin through the purges and the Second World War. After Stalin died he displaced Georgi Malenkov as leader for being insufficiently vigorous in pursuit of the Cold War. In February 1956 he rocked the communist world by denouncing Stalinism in a speech to the 20th Party Congress. While this encouraged a political thaw he cracked down ruthlessly on Hungary later that year. Thereafter he pursued a policy of peaceful co-existence with the West while boasting about Soviet military strength. He was undermined by a slowing economy, the United States pulling ahead in the missile race, the deepening split with China and his climb-down over Cuban missiles. He was ousted in October 1964.

Leonid Brezhnev (1906–82)

Led the Soviet Union for eighteen years after working his way up the Communist Party hierarchy. When he helped force Khrushchev out of office in 1964 he was already heir apparent. His determination to retain the party's power led him to resist calls for economic

liberalization and, in 1968, crush the 'Prague spring', leading to the enunciation of the 'Brezhnev doctrine', according to which socialist countries were allowed to intervene in each other's affairs when their 'essential common interests' were 'threatened by one of their number'. He built up Soviet military power while negotiating détente with the West. His policies led to economic stagnation and over-dependence on military strength, culminating in the invasion of Afghanistan in late 1979, by which time Brezhnev was ailing.

Yuri Andropov (1914–84)

Was in charge of the KGB (State Security Committee) from 1967 to 1982 when he became Soviet leader after Brezhnev's death. He was ambassador to Hungary during the 1956 uprising when he helped organize the Soviet invasion and the repression of dissidents. Although quick to consolidate his power as leader he soon became seriously ill and died after fifteen months in office.

Mikhail Gorbachev (1931–)

Had been a loyal party official, specializing in agriculture, when he became Soviet leader in 1985 following the death of Chernenko. He was expected to modernize the system, not abolish it, yet reforms opened up the system and he lost control. His embrace of radical arms control and withdrawal from Afghanistan gained him Western support but denied him the option of taking stern measures to resist the anti-communist movement that overtook Eastern Europe in 1989. By 1990 Germany was reunified and nationalist sentiment was gathering support even within the Soviet Union. During 1991 he lost his way, first breaking with the reformers but then finding himself under house arrest. The hard-line coup was defeated through the efforts of Boris Yeltsin, who eventually became the first leader of a Russia, after the Soviet Union was disbanded on Christmas Day 1991, with Gorbachev its last leader.

Chinese

Chiang Kai-shek (1887–1975)

Entered political life as part of the republican movement that overthrew China's Manchu dynasty. He used his power base in the Nationalist Party to expel communists, but then suspended this conflict after Japan invaded China in 1937. The communists were popularly seen to have been more committed in the fight against Japan and offered more to the peasantry, pushed the nationalists out of mainland China in 1949 to Taiwan. There Chiang established a dictatorship under American protection, with the hope of one day returning. Before his death American rapprochement with mainland China was already under way.

MAO TSE-TUNG (1893–1976)

Was a great revolutionary leader, effective against the Japanese and the n ationalists using the strategy of People's War. He was less successful in government, in part because of his naïve belief that the moral will of people could substitute for material support, especially in economic development. He was prepared to follow Stalin but not Khrushchev and this eventually led to an open rift with Moscow and an increasingly extreme, xenophobic, anti-bureaucratic and isolated path for China, culminating in the Cultural Revolution, intended to preserve the purity of the revolution and its rural roots, led to chaos.

DENG XIAOPING (1904–97)

Was a pragmatist in the Chinese Communist Party who suffered under the Cultural Revolution. He came back into favour in 1973 and was a protagonist in the power struggle with the radical 'gang of four'. By 1980 Deng was effectively in control, but worked through his supporters rather than take prominent posts for himself. He encouraged the modernization of the Chinese economy and improved relations with the West.

EUROPEANS

KONRAD ADENAUER (1876–1967)

Was the first chancellor of the Federal Republic of Germany. Until 1963 he steered his country firmly into the Western camp and membership of NATO. He was also a key figure in the formation of the European Economic Community and the reconciliation with France.

WILLY BRANDT (1913–92)

Was a German Social Democrat who was mayor of West Berlin through the crisis years. He became chairman of the SPD in 1964 and, after a period as vice-chancellor in a coalition from 1966, he became chancellor in 1969. He pursued an active foreign policy, working successfully to establish relations with the East. He was obliged to reign in 1974 when his aide, Günther Guillaume, was revealed to be an East German spy.

NICOLAE CEAUSESCU (1918–89)

Was the communist leader of Romania from 1965. An independent foreign policy for a time led him to get some favours from the West. Economic collapse and an ever more outrageous personality cult undermined his rule. When the wave of anti-communist reform swept communist Europe in 1989 he had few defences. He ordered troops to fire against demonstrators but by December he had lost support of the army and his opponents dominated the streets of Bucharest. On 22 December he and his wife were captured, summarily tried and shot.

CHARLES DE GAULLE (1890–1970)

Was leader of the Free French forces during the Second World War but grew frustrated with chaotic French politics. As a result of the Algerian crisis he set his own terms to become the first president of the Fifth Republic in 1958. By 1962 he had accepted Algeria as an independent state and became an increasingly discordant voice in the Atlantic alliance, arguing against American hegemony and pushing ahead with an independent nuclear deterrent. In 1966 he withdrew France from NATO's integrated military command. His efforts to develop an alternative security policy for Europe based on the European Economic Community and détente made little headway during his time in office.

MARGARET THATCHER (1925–)

Became Britain's first woman prime minister in 1979. Although her lasting legacy lay in domestic policy, she had an international reputation as a tough leader, forged during the 1982 Falklands War. She gratefully embraced a Russian denunciation as the 'Iron Lady' and took a strong anti-Soviet stance. Yet she was the first Western leader to recognize the potential of Gorbachev and the opportunities for loosening the Soviet hold on Eastern Europe. She lost efforts in 1990 because her cabinet was split on European policy.

JOSIP BROZ TITO (1892–1980)

Led the communist-dominated partisan movements that fought the Nazi occupation of Yugoslavia. After the war he consolidated his hold on Yugoslavian politics and pursued an independent foreign policy. Stalin attempted to purge him but this failed and led to the two countries falling out in what became the first major breach in the Soviet empire. As a result Tito opted for non-alignment between East and West. He tried also to pursue a middle course in economic policy. His greatest failure was not to provide a solution to the internal ethnic problems which exploded in Yugoslavia after his death.

FURTHER READING

I have inevitably drawn on my own research into contemporary conflicts and strategy. Those interested in following this up can find discussion of the key nuclear debates in *The Evolution of Nuclear Strategy*, 2nd edn (London: Macmillan for IISS, 1989), the crises of the early 1960s in *Kennedy's Wars: Berlin, Cuba, Laos and Vietnam* (New York: OUP, 2000), the Falklands War (with Virginia Gamba-Stonehouse) in *Signals of War: The Falklands Conflict of 1982* (London: Faber and Faber, 1990) and the Gulf War (with Efraim Karsh) in *The Gulf Conflict: 1990–91* (London: Faber and Faber, 1993).

The general literature on the Cold War is substantial. Some of the earlier works, which could not be based on archives, are still worth reading, including Louis Halle's *The Cold War as History* (New York, 1967) and two books by Adam Ulam, *The Rivals: America and Russia since World War II* (New York, 1972), and *Dangerous Relations* (New York, 1983). John Gaddis has produced consistently high quality histories of the Cold War. It is interesting to compare his *Strategy of Containment* (New York, 1982), on American policy after the Second World War, with his more recent *We Now Know: Rethinking Cold War History* (Oxford, 1997), which is able to take advantage of the Soviet archives that were made available after the end of the Cold War, taking the story into the crisis years of the early 1960s. The same period is covered, but from a Russian perspective, in Vladislav Zubok and Constantine Pleshakov, *Inside the Kremlin's Cold War: From Stalin to Khrushchev* (Cambridge, Mass., 1996). An early overview of the whole period by an experienced journalist is found in Martin Walker, *The Cold War* (London, 1993). Jeremy Isaacs and Taylor Downing. *Cold War* (London, 1998) was based on the CNN series. A thorough examination of the military dimensions of the conflict is Norman Friedman, *Fifty Year War: Conflict and Strategy in the Cold War* (Annapolis, MD, 1999). A lively but not wholly convincing analysis is Richard Ned Lebow and Janice Stein, *We All Lost the Cold War* (Princeton, 1994).

The origins are examined in all the general histories of the Cold War, but in detail in Melvin Leffler, *A Preponderance of Power: National Security, the Truman Administration, and the Cold War* (Stanford, 1992) and Daniel Yergin, *Shattered Peace: The Origins of the Cold War and the National Security State* (Boston, 1977). For a rich and evocative memoir by a key figure from the period see Dean Acheson, *Present at the Creation* (New York, 1969). The Berlin blockade is analysed by Avi Shlaim in *The United States and the Berlin Blockade* (Los Angeles, 1983). For discussions of Korea see Jon Halliday and Bruce Cumings, *Korea: The Unknown War* (London, 1988), and William Stueck, *The Korean War: An International History* (Princeton, 1995).

ARMS RACE

Two excellent books by Richard Rhodes describes the development of the atomic and hydrogen bombs and the policy debates that surrounded them: *The Making of the Atomic Bomb* (New York, 1986) and *Dark Sun: The Making of the Hydrogen Bomb* (New York, 1995). David Holloway's *Stalin and the Bomb*

(New Haven, 1994) remains the best study of Soviet nuclear developments. McGeorge Bundy was Kennedy's national security adviser. His history of the nuclear issue is particularly strong on the first two decades: *Danger and Survival: Choices About the Bomb in the First Fifty Years* (New York, 1988). For a racy discussion of the nuclear strategists see Fred Kaplan, *The Wizards of Armageddon* (New York, 1983). Thomas Schelling remains one of the most compelling writers on nuclear strategy and his *Arms and Influence* (New Haven, 1966) effectively conveys the paradoxical character of strategic thinking in the early 1960s. A. C. Bacevich, *The Pentomic Era: The US Army between Korea and Vietnam* (Washington DC, 1986) describes effectively the problems of the US Army in coping with tactical nuclear weapons.

CRISIS MANAGEMENT

Michael Beschloss, *Kennedy v. Khrushchev* (London, 1991) provides a blow-by-blow account of the crisis years. A lively account of the Berlin crisis is found in Ann Tusa, *The Last Division: Berlin and the Wall* (London, 1996). There is an immense literature on Cuba, but two standard texts now are the riveting transcripts of meetings conducted by Kennedy during the crisis found in Ernest R. May and Philip D. Zelikow, *The Kennedy Tapes: Inside the White House During the Cuban Missile Crisis* (Cambridge, Mass., 1997) and an account which draws deeply on Soviet archives, Aleksandr Fursenko and Timothy Naftali, 'One Hell of a Gamble': The Secret History of the Cuban Missile Crisis* (New York, 1997). Scott Sagan, *The Limits of Safety: Organizations, Accidents, and Nuclear Weapons* (Princeton, NJ, 1993) is a sobering account of the hidden dangers of the nuclear years. The post-Cuba debates on nuclear strategy and flexible response are covered by two insiders in Alain Enthoven and Wayne Smith, *How Much is Enough? Shaping the Defense Program, 1961–69* (New York, 1971) and by an academic in Jane Stromseth, *The Origins of Flexible Response: NATO's Debate over Strategy in the 1960s* (London, 1988).

VIETNAM

On the theory and practice of guerrilla warfare see Daniel Moran's contribution to this series, *Wars of National Liberation* (London, 2001). A good account of the American fascination with counter-insurgency is Douglas Blaufarb's *The Counter-Insurgency Era* (New York, 1977). For a feel of the impact that this had on policy-making on Vietnam see David Halberstam's *The Best and the Brightest* (New York, 1972). Chester Cooper, *The Lost Crusade: America in Vietnam* (New York, 1970), is a vivid memoir of early American policy-making. The communist side is covered by William Duiker in *The Communist Road to Power in Vietnam* (Boulder, Col., 1996). One of the most critical figures on the American side, Robert S. McNamara, tells his controversial side of the story with Brian Vandemark in *In Retrospect: The Tragedy and Lessons of Vietnam* (New York, 1995). Another controversial retrospect is Harry G. Summers's *On Strategy: A Critical Analysis of the Vietnam War* (Novato, Calif., 1982). The Nixon period is covered in Jeffrey Kimball, *Nixon's Vietnam War* (Lawrence, Kan., 1998).

DÉTENTE

The full flavour of superpower diplomacy in the 1970s, including Vietnam, is found in the readable but very long volumes of memoirs of Henry Kissinger, *The White House Years* (Boston, Mass., 1979), *Years of Upheaval* (Boston, Mass.,

1982) and *Years of Renewal* (New York, 1999). An intriguing insight into Kissinger's methods can be found in William Burr (ed.), *Kissinger Transcripts : The Top Secret Talks With Beijing and Moscow* (New York, 1999). NATO's debates about its conventional forces are covered in John Duffield, *Power Rules: The Evolution of NATO's Conventional Force Posture* (Stanford, Calif., 1995). A fictional account by a senior military figure captures much of the thinking and assumptions of the late 1970s and early 1980s: General Sir John Hackett, *The Third World War: The Untold Story* (London, 1982). See also Christopher Bellamy, *The Evolution of Modern Land Warfare: Theory and Practice* (London, 1990).

THE LESSONS OF WAR
The Arab–Israeli wars are well covered (much better than the Indo-Pakistani) in such works as Ahron Bregman and Jihan El-Tahri, *The Fifty Years War: Israel and the Arabs* (London, 1998), prepared in association with a BBC series, and Chaim Herzog, *The Arab–Israeli Wars: War and Peace in the Middle East, from the War of Independence through Lebanon* (New York, 1982). Lebanon is covered from an Israeli perspective in Ze'ev Schiff and Ehud Ya'ari, *Israel's Lebanon War* (London, 1986), and from an American in Ralph Hallenback, *Military Force as an Instrument of U.S. Foreign Policy: Intervention in Lebanon, August 1982 – February 1984* (New York, 1991). On the Falklands, Max Hastings and Simon Jenkins, *The Battle for the Falklands* (London, 1983) remains remarkably reliable. For the Iran–Iraq War see Shahram Chubin and Charles Tripp, *Iran and Iraq at War* (London, 1988). A good account of Russia's troubles in Afghanistan is Mark Galeotti, *Afghanistan: The Soviet Union's Last War* (London, 1994).

THE END OF THE COLD WAR
The most substantial accounts of the periods from the start of détente to the end of the Cold War have been provided by Raymond Garthoff, following a distinguished career in government. These are *Détente and Confrontation* (rev. edn) and *The Great Transition: American Soviet Relations and the End of the Cold War* (both Washington, DC, 1994). The sense of the deterioration of superpower relations in the early 1980s is found in Fred Halliday's *The Making of the Second Cold War* (London, 1983), while revelations about the first Reagan administration's approach to nuclear arms control are found in Strobe Talbott, *Deadly Gambits: The Reagan Administration and the Stalemate in Nuclear Arms Control* (New York, 1984). Frances Fitzgerald, *Way Out There in the Blue,* (New York, 2000) is the story of Star Wars, but is also a profound look at Reagan's whole approach to the Cold War. There are a number of accounts of the end of the Cold War. An important memoir is George H. W. Bush and Brent Scowcroft, *A World Transformed,* (New York, 1998). See also Michael Beschloss and Strobe Talbott, *At the Highest Levels: The Inside Story of the End of the Cold War* (Boston, 1993). Gabriel Partos, *The World that Came in from the Cold* (London, 1993), provides a lively account of the collapse of the Soviet empire based on interviews conducted for a radio series. The consequences of the end of the Cold War for the Soviet military are examined in William Odom, *The Collapse of the Soviet Military* (New Haven, 1998). Post-war nuclear issues are debated by Scott Sagan and Kenneth N. Waltz in *The Spread of Nuclear Weapons: A Debate* (New York, 1995).

INDEX

Figures in *italic* refer to captions

PICTURE CREDITS

Every effort has been made to contact the copyright holders for images reproduced in this book. The publishers would welcome any errors or omissions being brought to their attention.

ENDPAPER: *Soviet naval units marching in Red Square parade.*